A BOTCHER IN FRANCE

A BOTCHER IN FRANCE

Getting it Wrong the Easy Way

Trevor Danby

Illustrations by Emma Danby

Book Guild Publishing
Sussex, England

First published in Great Britain in 2007 by
The Book Guild Ltd
Pavilion View
19 New Road
Brighton
BN1 1UF

Typesetting in Times by
IML Typographers, Birkenhead, Merseyside

Printed in Great Britain by
CPI Antony Rowe

A catalogue record for this book is available from
The British Library.

ISBN 978 1 84624 169 7

Contents

Preface

If Michelangelo had known the consequences to his health would he have started the ceiling? If Scott had known of his frozen end, would he have started for the South Pole? Would I have chased my modest dream of owning a small piece of peasant heritage in France, if I had known the labour and cost involved?

Chasing a dream without knowing what one is getting into leads to hard lessons down dangerous roads. A sense of the ridiculous can see you through.

Acknowledgements

Love and heart-felt thanks to:

Kate for her astute criticism and persistent resistance to my obstinate belief that my first drafts were indelible.

Liz, not only for her radiant picture of the house, but also for her honest and forthright editing skill.

Emma for her illustrations and for long hours spent with Chris in front of the computer screen to give coherent shape to the text with skills quite beyond me.

Also, I thank everyone who became a character in the book and would have them know they have enriched my life in inestimable ways. I leave them to admit to their identities, or not, as they may wish, but my last word must be that I proceeded, throughout, on the principle that exaggeration is the best way to tell the story and, in the end, gets nearest the truth.

1

In for a Penny ...

Lounging in front of the telly, feet out, face buried in rustling Sunday broadsheets, I came across a French advert for cheap property in the Poitou-Charente region in the south-west of France. If I was to believe the agent, buildings were to be had at ridiculously low prices in what he described as the second sunniest region in France.

Since I insisted upon taking the family on a cultural tour of that country every summer, it seemed no inconvenience at all to call in on him when next we visited the region to take our usual cultural interest in Cognac and to stock up on the product to which the town lent its name.

I arranged a meeting on the phone and weeks later we turned up with more curiosity than expectation. I lost no time in testing his claims, and was pleasantly surprised to find he was willing and able to furnish me with information about several properties, comprising farmhouses with barns and other small buildings suitable for renovation at well under twenty thousand pounds.

It turned out that the agent I had first made contact with was the front man, responsible for placing the adverts in English newspapers. The real power behind the publicity was a corpulent French woman, who proved to be the most enthusiastic vendor it has ever been my qualified privilege to meet.

There was not a single property on her books that was not incredibly 'beeeyooteefoool', with unrivalled opportunities for

1

improvement, culminating in nothing less than manorial splendour. Every hovel she showed us had the makings of a palace. She would verbally transform them to her own satisfaction with the consummate ease of an illusionist, except that her flights of fancy were delivered so rapidly that most of it went over our heads. Nothing was said about the cost, apart from a dismissive wave of the hand indicating it to be a mere trifle.

Eventually, exhausted by superlatives, we discreetly asked if we could be left to visit properties on our own, and since most of them were miles apart, she seemed amenable to the suggestion. In the next three days we saw fifteen different properties, but encountered nothing that seemed appropriate. Many were impressive in terms of the amount of real estate and land you got for your money, but generally frightening in their obvious demands on time and purse to make habitable.

I finally drummed up courage to hand an ultimatum to Madame. I stood before her and in a shoulder-shrugging, fidgety, childlike way, suggested she might be able to find us 'a detached house on the edge of a small village offering amenities, with an uninterrupted view from a garden, large enough to ask for serious landscaping but small enough to be manageable – oh, and requiring renovation – and therefore cheap'.

Embarrassment had made me deliver all this at break-neck speed. If I expected the agent to dance with glee at the prospect, I was to be disappointed. She returned my quizzical stare with an impassive look, loaded with subtext. I retained a modicum of dignity and informed her I was going over to La Rochelle for a long weekend and if, in the meantime, anything of the kind I had outlined came up, I would be interested. With glazed eyes, and compressed lips, she said she would look around.

'Yeah, yeah, yeah!' I thought. I thanked her and walked stiffly out of the shop, believing I had just burned a boat with no return ticket.

Three days later, the family squeezed into a telephone kiosk; two adults, a student daughter just turned twenty-one, and a lanky

seventeen-year-old son, resembling a scrum practice for the summer sales. I took a deep breath and dialled the agent's number. The agent picked up the phone with a, 'Can I 'elp yeeou?'

Was there, I reminded her, the faintest chance that she might have found something that conceivably approximated to any of the requirements I had put to her? The pause was filled with the rustling of papers, and then her voice came back with a hint of disdainful reserve.

'I 'ave a leetle ouse that per'aps will be wat you are seeking for, but I don' know if it is so.'

'What is it?' I asked, ready to disguise my scepticism.

'Eet is in fine place, with a view *extraordinaire* over the village.'

'Really?' I said. It was a reasonable enough start. I placed my hand over the receiver to relay the information that followed. More rustling at the other end, and then, in a voice that suggested she would much rather be filing her nails, she said, 'Eet 'as a larj gaarden weeth looverly view, and the 'ouse ees varee, varee old.'

I nodded affirmatively and repeated, '*Oui, oui*,' as my wife, Kate, plucked at my sleeve impatiently. 'Very, very old house,' I repeated as I continued to nod. 'In need of tender loving care. Yes, of course. Tomorrow?' I put the thumb up for the family. 'Good, we'll be there.' I hung up.

'Only one way to find out if it's any good,' I said, hope struggling with scepticism. My family were a patient bunch, and restricted their resistance to low mutters.

Inspecting a property in opalescent light under sunny blue skies, with nature beaming at you in sight and sound, is a

3

wonderful experience I can recommend to everybody. The crickets chirruping, the heat shimmering and the leaves fluttering gently in the wind, while you chew a freshly picked ear of corn, make for an idyllic experience.

Unfortunately, the day we went to inspect our little hovel, it was chucking it down cats and dogs. Looking through the windscreen was like peering through a rippled bathroom window after a steaming hot shower. Far from being a 'shorts, sandals and sunglasses' sort of day, it was a 'wellington boots and trench coat' one; the kind that never features in the tourist brochures, or even your worst nightmares. We were totally unprepared and could only muster hats made of supermarket bags and shower-resistant plastic macs. Umbrellas were irrelevant; the wind would have carried you away.

'Eet is navar like thees! Eet ees *extraordinaire!*' our guide insisted. Certainly it was beyond our experience, hopefully alien to the region, and possibly beyond living memory. The windscreen wipers did a dervish dance with the horizontal rain, as we followed the agent's car. Huge branches waved menacingly over us, to the accompaniment of dancing hedgerows, all shouting at us.

'Get the heck out of it!' they yelled. 'This is no playground for tourists! You need roots as old as folklore to live here!'

When you are hell bent on folly, you are not dissuaded by a mere mother and father of a downpour coming off the Atlantic from going to see the 'bargain of the season', when you should be building an ark. You are not to be diverted even if the sky falls in.

The first sight of the *belle propriété*, as we wound slowly down the lane, was less than entrancing. We were confronted by a pair of dilapidated slatted wooden gates, leaning away from their hinges like two drunken veterans. They looked as if they might have been painted green at one time. It was not a good omen, and I consciously ignored my family's silence, as we got out of the car and took stock of the scene with baleful eyes. To the left of the gate was a gutter-less barn bereft of facade. From its roof poured torrents of water. To the right was a concrete ramp disappearing into a black tunnel of vines and wisteria.

The agent kicked open the gates and led us down this slope with a happy and wholly incomprehensible abandon. She was one of those souls who cover all misgivings with optimism, especially where there is an outside chance of a sale.

We crouched down to duck under the wisteria, and our attention was divided between trying to prevent water from invading our collars and attempting to keep our feet from losing their grip on the slippery surface. The path ended at a sombre courtyard where, as the cold water trickled down our spines, we could dimly make out the front door of the house, fronted by a pair of manure-brown metal shutters and a single window covered by a heavy green wooden one.

Madame smiled and nodded constant affirmation, as if offering an antidote to the appalling weather. Hunched under her rain-bonnet, resembling Darth Vader, she told us in the hushed tones of a museum curator of the wonderful opportunities that we could not fail to appreciate as soon as we entered this property. She fumbled with a large bunch of keys, and shook the lock out of its coma, making it emit a shrill squeak, as if suddenly surprised to be alive.

'*Voilà!*' she exclaimed, with the same cheerful confidence, bodily shoving the door open. She entered the blackness, swinging her keys like a Dickensian gaoler. A quick flick of a wall switch established there was no electricity, whereupon our guide tramped through to a second room and, with noisy gusto, opened a shutter to let in the murky light that hung reluctantly back. As we ducked under the door lintel, reminded that all French peasants were only four foot six tall, a stale mustiness met us.

As our eyes adjusted to the murk, we realised we had entered a junk shop full of wardrobes and beds, all draped with dust sheets, ready for very brave and exhausted folk to sleep in. The wardrobes stood side by side, like huge sentry boxes. Madame beckoned us into the far room, and pronounced it a bedroom.

There was nothing to distinguish it from the first room, as it was equally cluttered with wardrobes and beds. A single window was set in a recess, shedding enough light to reveal all the cobwebs, grime and dust. I asked how long the house had been unoccupied. Apparently the owner was a widow, and had left to enter a retirement home.

'So she is an old lady, is she?' I enquired.

'Well, she is … not able to look after herself,' was the evasive reply.

'Her sons thought it best to have her looked after,' she added, with a hint of something sinister. I had visions of negotiating with an absent-minded bed and wardrobe collector, constrained on both sides by two male attendants wearing dark expressions, dark glasses and white overalls.

It may have been the sceptical look on all our faces, but Madame launched into a rigmarole which included the propositions that, first, the house was in very good condition, second, one could live in it while renovating, and, finally, the whole thing could be done for a song. We smiled and nodded, and left it there.

I pointed to a trapdoor in the floor, and asked where it led to. Madame bent down and pulled it up by an iron ring, whereupon a sweet damp odour swept upwards, and I found myself peering down into an inky void. Everyone turned to look at me, and, as if I had to prove something, I began to descend a precipitous ladder, (which I later learned had the unmerited name of 'miller's staircase') into this murky dungeon. I waved my arm about me in a frantic effort to rid myself of shrouds of cobwebs, hoping earnestly that they were not inhabited.

My brave family peered over the rim at me. When my eyes had adjusted to the gloom, I was able to tell them of rows of empty rabbit hutches, of cattle rings set in the wall, a vast army of bottles with unidentifiable contents, and ferns growing out of the wall.

'There are what look like the bones of some unfortunate prisoner kept here for years,' I added, just to bring the questions to a stop. I beat as hasty a retreat from the ghouls and beasties as dignity would allow. (Later that evening, in the best tradition of story telling, I would exaggerate the horrors to make my bravery properly appreciated.) I asked the agent where the toilet facilities were.

'*Pas de problème*. There is everything you need!' was the immediate response. With a triumphant gesture, she led the way out of the door and pointed to a breeze-block lean-to at the end of the house. I scuttled as fast as I could to the door of this appurtenance under the inefficient protection of Madame's umbrella.

She ushered me in like a doorman of the Savoy Hotel. (For Savoy, substitute a hut with unpainted door on rusty hinges.) I entered and waited for my irises to enlarge. Gradually, a rectangular cell came into focus, containing a plank laid across two low pillars over a cavernous hole. From the rotting beams hung huge cobwebs with arachnids of gigantic proportions. The most pressing need my bowels or bladder might urge me to attend to would not induce me to enter this hell-hole. I escaped with a shudder.

Leaving the dubious benefit of Madame's guidance, I walked to the end of the house and looked at the garden. It was all on the incline, and would make a wonderful dry-ski slope. Did I say 'dry'? Hardly!

Once in the house again, I sauntered over to the far window and looked down on the village below. The ancient abbey church, the line of poplars along the river bank, and the road that followed the curve of the valley all contributed to a kind of dismal beauty.

The agent was watching me closely, like a panther ready to spring. My family, giving an impression of a group intent on collective suicide, shifted their weights, sniffed, shivered and, in every other subtle way, conveyed their feelings about the whole visit.

Madame held her quizzical gaze, deciphering my body language, as the wardrobes leant over us and the beds gathered round. A moment of foot-scuffing, an exchange of covert looks beneath beetled brows and I said, 'We'll have it.'

2

It's Like This, Your Honour ...

There is little point in anyone conducting a post-mortem of an irreversible process. This is especially true when you cannot even explain it to yourself. In any case, 'Don't get off the roller coaster once it's started,' as they say.

However, when you have unpremeditatedly done something as big as buying an old shell of a building you have to ask yourself some questions. I was certainly excited at owning the place, but wasn't sure what it all meant. How could I justify it? To what purpose could I put it? Was this a form of escape? Was it a desperate attempt to structure time, a mid-life crisis? It would certainly give us lots to do, but, at the end of the day, I just did not know.

I may have been foolhardy, but not enough to believe all I had been told by the agent. All that huffing and puffing and optimistic dismissal of problems was codswallop. Even I could recognise that, sooner rather than later the roof would have to be given additional support and strength. It might even need to be replaced. In any case, if the roof space was to be at all habitable, the cross-beam would have to be removed, otherwise we would be permanently bent over at right-angles moving from one end to the other. The cellar was also a potential nightmare, and raised up all kinds of images to disturb the mind. It was only a damp cellar for animals and rabbit hutches, but what had gone on down there, down the ages, in that damp, sinister space? Damp? Oh, yes, was it damp. I was soon to find out just how damp that was!

When all the signing of papers had finished, we left the agent to look into such matters. The first thing was to procure a good architect to oversee the external alterations and to ensure they complied with the bureaucratic requirements for the preservation of regional style and compliance in a listed village.

Lots of letters began to fly back and forth across the Channel. There was good news and bad news. The good was that the house was considered to be very old and therefore its external shape worth preserving for posterity. That meant that any fabric added on had to be set back from the existing building in order to show clearly the boundary of the original building.

I supported all these regulations, and was ready to fork out the funds to ensure they were complied with, for I really wanted to return character to this unprepossessing edifice: someone had gone to a lot of trouble to plant it there way back in the mists of heaven knows when. The walls at the base were around four to five feet thick in places! The single recessed window dominating the valley had the best view of the village and road in both directions.

It was a featureless building, and not typical of most Charentais farmhouses (most of which were low extended dwellings with a large barn often adjacent and attached to them), but it had a fine view and an attractive and exclusive position that suited us down to the ground, even though it was of the sloping kind.

My wife and I egged each other on to believe that the house had seen the sixteenth-century religious wars and even medieval wars with the English in its time. How could it be otherwise, when there had been an eleventh-century abbey in the valley? Wasn't the church the remaining proof of this? I reined in these thoughts for a second or two when I remembered that buildings hadn't changed their style over several hundreds of years, so it was well-nigh impossible to date it, but who wanted to hear that?

Whatever the case, we wanted to be careful not to make radical changes that would detract from the hidden history of the place. It was as well to keep in the locals' good books and try to give the

Brits a good name. How did we know if they had forgiven us for all those medieval English marauders and their mercenaries? Had they yet put behind them the worst excesses of the Black Prince, who, as recently as 1370, had sacked, looted and raped with abandon in the town of Limoges, just across the departmental border?

Come to think about it, better not remind them of Waterloo, Trafalgar, the Duke of Marlborough and Quebec. Better not transgress their laws, or it could stir it all up again. Nor did we want to upset any household ghosts that might be hanging around.

'Remember,' we told ourselves, 'we don't own the house. We're merely holding it in trust for our French friends in the new united Europe. How can we seriously suppose that we own a grain of French earth in the scheme of time's swift passage?' We worked ourselves up into wonderful self-approval, just thinking of all the altruistic good we were about to embark on.

One morning a letter came telling us that the changes we proposed, though acceptable to the Beaux-Arts Architectural Department in Paris, would cost considerably more than we had envisaged. It was essential that we carefully retain the regional style, because the house lay equidistant between the eleventh-century church and the *Lanterne des Morts*, which stood in the cemetery. Tourists visiting the village would have to pass our house on the way from one to the other, and nobody wanted them passing an eyesore, did they?

This *Lanterne des Morts* was news to us. What were we talking about here? It turned out that the locals were especially proud of this particular specimen, one of the best examples of its kind in the Poitou-Charentes. No bones about it, it was significant historical stuff, dating from the twelfth century. We worked out that the nearest translation for it was, probably, 'Beacon to the Dead'. It consisted of a monolithic column built on a stepped stone plinth, of a type found in cemeteries and various elevated sites throughout the region, and is believed to have been lit up at burial services to send the dead on their way to paradise. All rather theatrical in its way, but no doubt capable of bringing a little cheer to otherwise sombre proceedings.

It is also posited that, because they are erected on an elevated site, these beacons could well have been lit to alert the surrounding inhabitants to the approaching rampages of the Black Prince and his English hell-hounds. Oh, come on, this was getting paranoid! Why would the English be singled out? The Navarrais, the Bretons, the Gascons and even the Spanish were traipsing all over France doing much the same thing during the fourteenth century. Apparently, in those embattled times, the villagers would herd themselves into fortified churches, some of which had ditches round them for protection. There were even machines of war housed in the bell towers to repel intruders. If you were too late to gain entry to the church (it was first come, first served) then you would be forced to flee to the quarries, woods and even small islands in the middle of the rivers, shipping as many cattle and other chattels with you on flat-bottomed boats.

But I digress. Now, in the last years of the twentieth century, our struggle was with the bureaucrats. Responding to the information supplied by our architect, I decided I had better travel down and meet him on site to discuss the full import of the bureaucrats' demands face to face. And meet we did, standing side by side in the garden of the house on a crisp November morning, under an opalescent sky and with the warm sun stroking our backs as we gazed down on the village.

Monsieur, the architect, had a dapper appearance that you could have mistaken for English. He was attentive and polite, and said pleasant things about my amateurish attempt to capture my vision on paper, which clearly showed him to be cultured. Having diplomatically got that out of the way, he took from his briefcase his impressions of what he thought I might have been aiming to convey to him. His pen and wash drawings breathed instant character and soul into the original shape. The windows were eyes for an old, blind house to look out onto the twentieth century, without destroying the character of the main body.

What a joy to share the vision, and to hear him say that light would stream into the house from every direction; that a proper drainage system would be laid, not only gathering our effluent in a civilised and private fashion, but enriching the soil of the sloping garden with an intricate arrangement of pipes. Even greater relief and joy to hear that the lean-to toilet, with its infernal altar to obscene arachnids, would be razed to the ground, and a shower room made an integral part of the house!

This splendid gentleman shared my delight in the prospect of the garden, as we stood there admiring the view. We nodded, smiling, and breathing in the champagne air. What an optimistic frame of mind it put one in! A moment's pause to savour the vision of the future, and then he turned to me and said, in a matter of fact, but self-conscious tone, 'And what, Monsieur, do you propose to do with the stream in the cellar?'

'Stream? What stream?' I turned to see a slight pucker in the corner of his mouth, as he raised a quizzical eyebrow a millimetre. I tossed the word around, and repeated it inside my head a few times, but could honestly say it meant nothing to me. I said it aloud a couple of times, but it obdurately refused to make sense of itself.

'You know nothing about it?' he said in the tone of an under-rehearsed actor expressing innocent surprise.

'About what? A stream?'

'*Mon dieu!*' he muttered with simulated passion. 'That is quite a thing.'

'Is it?' I muttered back.

He gathered a cloak of polite kindness round him, nodding sympathetically, as he turned to me.

'Well, well. There you are, then. I thought they had told you.'

I stood, resolutely refusing to prompt him any more from the wings. He continued, blustering a little.

'Well whatever you will do with the *cave*, you must be sure to let it flow freely.'

'Flow?'

'But, yes. You must allow the stream to flow through the cave, or the damp will rise up the walls.'

'Flow through the ...?'

'*Allons-y!*' he said suddenly, 'Let's go. You must see it.'

I needed no urging. See it I must, obviously.

We skied down the dew-covered ground at the side of the house, mercifully without landing on our buttocks. Monsieur the Architect pushed the rotting wide planked door open, strode into the black interior and played a small torch, which he took from his coat pocket, on the rear wall. Leaving aside the rabbit hutches and battalion of bottles arrayed on the rocky outcrop on which the house had been founded, he played the beam on numerous vertical streaks of green moss and algae left behind by rivulets of water. Monsieur was extremely taken with the sight, and became very voluble about it.

'You see, when it rains, this becomes a stream. The house is built on the rocky substrata. The rain comes,' – and here he began, with his fingers, to helpfully mime the rain falling – 'it descends

through the soil, seeps slowly through the clay, and gathers on the rock beneath, where it can fall no further ... ' He smiled like a magician who is about to complete the conjuring trick, 'except to follow the surface of the sloping rock and enter the cellar here.'

His smile evaporated, and he added earnestly, 'If it would rain now you could see it very well.'

He sounded disappointed that he couldn't illustrate this, and I nodded sympathetically. He brightened up, and said, 'But, as soon as the next downpour comes, you will see it, yes?'

I nodded again, without sharing his enthusiasm. He was in full flow, even if the stream wasn't. Obviously he needed to prod my interest with more underlining facts.

'The ground all around slopes, and so all the rain will sooner or later ooze out here. And so, *voilà!* It is evidence that you have a house on very firm foundations!'

I energised my mouth into a faintly appreciative smile at having such fine foundations, while still thinking hard about the stream. Monsieur saw this as a privilege, while I was feeling, let us say, 'less certain' about the consequences of the feature.

Builders of yore were very happy to lay their foundations on rock, and ready to live with the damp, especially when it was their beasts that had to endure the worst of it, chained down there in the *cave*. In any case, life expectancy was such that you would be taken from the worldly scene before rheumatoid arthritis set in. Many French still live with it today – the damp, not arthritis – and nobody is going to spend good money on a surveyor in order to hear there is damp climbing up the wall, when he knows it already. Today there are excellent modern ways of efficiently insulating it anyway. In 'them far off days', they probably dreamt of dry walls, and talked about them like we talk about the weather.

Instead of, 'Hullo, Jean, nice day, isn't it?' Pierre would have said, 'Nice dry walls, Jean.'

'Indeed, Pierre. Damp only a foot high today. By the end of the week, I reckon the lizards'll be clamberin' all over them walls again.'

Well, any such conjecture on my part would get nothing done – that was for sure.

But I was not prepared for the wonderful visions Monsieur the Architect had ready for me. He began by assuring me that there was no problem that could not be solved.

'Thank heavens,' I said.

Apparently, it all came down to containing the flow in a culvert and directing it out of the cellar through under-floor pipes. These would be covered by a plastic membrane encased in concrete. I expressed my gratitude for such assurance, and he took this as implicit agreement that a programme, more appropriate to Pharaoh's tomb, should begin immediately. He waxed lyrical about his vision; said he would design it for me, and I would marvel. His feet were lifting off the ground as he spoke, and so was the potential cost. I listened, but, all the while, looked for the gentlest way to bring him down to earth. I cut in on a short pause.

'*Oui, oui, Monsieur*. It all sounds magnificent. Unfortunately, I have to work within a budget.'

'*Mais, oui, Monsieur*, but it is always better, and cheaper, to have the work all done at the same time, while you have the artisans with you.'

'*Mais, oui*, but I can only release money as it becomes available.'

'*Mais oui!* But it is better to borrow the money and pay it off as soon as possible.'

This chess game could have gone on for some time, so I sent the queen out to check further attack.

'I have got x thousand francs to spend, and not a penny more.'

He was halted in his tracks. I could see the skid marks of his imagination on his face. He was rendered mute. The game was over. He conceded defeat. He nodded sadly, like a champion who has lost to a mere amateur.

'That is a pity, Monsieur,' he said, in a tone that suggested the city would fall to the enemy through the failure of funds. He had not the heart to continue further, except to reach agreement about how much could be done within my means.

To me it was an incredible amount of work for the money I offered. The entrepreneurs would build a bathroom, break through the metre-thick walls to integrate it, insert five new windows, and provide a new door to the *cave*, as well as installing a complete drainage system with septic tank, all for probably half what it would cost in England. This was all guaranteed by a *devis*, so long as we had the work done within the next six months. A word about this *devis* – it is a marvellous thing. It is, in effect, an estimate of the cost, but laid down in great detail. It is not an approximation. It is the actual cost and as such is binding on both parties, and must be honoured to the letter. Nothing in England comes anywhere near it for peace of mind. As it was, I was able also to look at all the work costs calculated, and draw a line under the place to which my finances permitted me to go. The builder would, therefore, complete the work that lay within the cost I had agreed to and leave me to do the rest.

I shook hands with Monsieur the Architect and we parted company, I being the happier and wiser, and he just the wiser.

There was one small item at the end of the agreed work to be done, which I thought not worth agreeing to, considering the cost involved. This was the removal off-site of the debris created by inserting the windows and demolishing the lean-to. I considered this to be unnecessary and, in any case, wanted to retain all that wonderful limestone to create garden features.

Monsieur the Architect seemed surprised at this, and asked me if I was quite sure. I made an affirmative plea for it all to be left on site. He shrugged, and handed me a copy of the plans, saying, 'To show your wife and children, Monsieur.'

We shook hands and he drove away up the lane, leaving a satisfied customer behind. I felt sure the stream could be sorted out. The French had lived with it for at least four hundred years. When the builder had done his part it would be child's play, we decided, and my wife and I began to apportion the tasks that would put our stamp on our very own small parcel of France.

One of God's greatest gifts is to keep us in ignorance of the future, to help us cope with the present. Total ignorance even makes challenges seem an attractive prospect. I was grateful for the ignorance that preceded what faced us the following spring.

3

Jungle Bombsite

The winter passed slowly, and French bureaucracy kept pace with it. After several unanswered requests for information, we began to think everyone had gone into hibernation, until Monsieur the Architect suddenly came back to us with the good news that our building alterations had finally been approved. He was proud to announce that the plans had been sent by Monsieur the Maire to the local '*Equip-ement*', whence they had gone to
the planning department of the regional capital, Angoulême, to be approved and then to the central department responsible for Architecture of Les Beaux Arts in Paris. Having travelled upstream, they had come downstream again, rubber-stamped all the way.

Monsieur the Architect was now pleased and proud to be able to instruct the builders to start. What a wonderful machine is run by French civil servants!

Hardly had we recovered from this phenomenon when, three weeks later, we received another letter notifying us that the work had been completed!

'What on earth ...' we exclaimed. This was unbelievable! All that work done in three weeks? The builder must have been crouched at the starting block and had a workforce the like of which you could only dream about. The letter was unequivocal, however.

'All has been completed to full satisfaction. I beg you to be willing to send the full payment with the least delay.'

My goodness, you had to hand it to those French workers! They were obviously used to making up for the bureaucratic delays. They had rolled up their sleeves and dug in to the work with unrivalled gusto!

'Good for them! Vive the French workers!'

I had already had thoughts of making another pilgrimage, and this sealed the intention. Chaucer's birds that 'slepen al the night with open eye' had nothing on me but, despite sleep deprivation, I became markedly more cheerful and pleasant to those around me. There was a rhythmic bounce in my bathroom songs, and I showed a pleasant face to the world. I ignored sideways glances that implied irrational behavioural patterns. I was excited by visions of a handsome new residence, at which the local community would cast admiring looks. We had spent all winter browsing over photographs, and conjecturing. Now I was to see the results in all their glory for the first time.

My lady decided she would come to share the joyful revelation, only if we took our old caravan down to provide creature comforts. So we hitched up and took off.

The day we arrived was one of joyful anticipation and heart-stirring spring warmth. The world was a wonderful place, especially this part of it. Bird song and crickets' chirping rose to a glorious sky as we turned the the top of the lane for the final few yards to the property.

Then, as we freewheeled down the hill, the dream we carried began to slip away like a kite from a child's grasp. There was a confusing distortion of the anticipated mental image, a complete betrayal of our rose-coloured vision. We drew up to the gate and gazed with disbelief.

To start with, you could not see the garden. You could hardly even see the gates. The weeds and shrubs were making a daylight escape. No sneak undercover break-out for *this* garden. It was shouting its liberty, like an angry mob of protestors on the march. Baby weeds had grown into adult bushes glaring at us on tip-toe. Feathery grasses thrust their head-dresses aggressively through the slats. Wisteria tendrils waved mockingly. If allowed to escape they could rouse up the whole of the Charente in another French Revolution against the British invaders.

We were struck dumb except for grunts and sighs. I suppressed my curses, but promised to release them later. Pushing the gate open, I was presented with further resistance. The tunnel beneath the wisteria descending to the house reminded me of a set for 'Orpheus in the Underworld'. It was completely overgrown, and strewn with a thick carpet of leaves that shifted perilously under foot. Peasants from ages past leered at us from behind the shrubbery, nodding gleefully at the fears of things to come. The fears were well founded on visible signs. The metal shutters gaped open, the latch forced, the lock broken, the door-jamb splintered. And the glass door stood ajar, whimpering and begging us to enter. Light streamed cruelly in through the new windows onto the heaped rubble, broken plaster and clods of clay. The house cringed away but the sun played its relentless searchlight everywhere. One of the stones prised from the wall to create the window opening had fallen and split one of the oak floorboards. My intuition led me to the window overlooking the village, perversely seeking the worst.

I was not disappointed. Below in the bottom garden was a scene of utter desolation, like the aftermath of an artillery bombardment. Huge rocks and rubble lay scattered where the builders had allowed them to roll down the slope, when they cut out the window surrounds. To the far left were avalanches of clay and stone from the excavations made for the septic tank. Next to this were broken tiles, breeze-blocks and lengths of worm-eaten rafters, remnants of the demolished lean-to. Paintings by Paul

21

Nash of the Western Front in the Imperial War Museum came to mind, as I sought to find some explanation for a scene of such devastating proportions.

It took some time before I could release my confused mind from the questions of what had caused this to happen, to settle on what was to be done about it. How could I restore the situation to some kind of sanity and order, and when would I find the time to do it?

The first move was obvious; have a cup of tea. She of the caravan was already ahead of my thoughts and had gone to put the kettle on. Soon we were cradling cups on our hands and were able to take some stock of the situation with the help of this symbol of comforting domesticity.

Reason gradually returned and I began to unravel the tangled thoughts fuelled by resentment. We began to voice the questions and follow them with possible theories. The builders had left the rubble exactly where it had fallen; that was for sure.

'Why would they leave everything like this?' asked my better half.

'How could the architect have come to the conclusion that everything was finished to satisfaction?' I added. 'To whose satisfaction? Certainly not mine.'

I was beginning to vent exultant anger but, at the back of my mind, there was something nagging away, scrabbling up the slope of the subconscious to reach the light of day. In a flash of enlightenment it dawned on me, as the memory of the *devis* I had signed returned to me.

'How will you take on all this extra work?' asked she. Her question niggled at me. Why did I resent it?

'You'll have to get on to the architect and have him round to see this mess,' she went on.

'Yes, yes, no doubt. And what will he say?' I replied in a half-distracted way.

'Well, I should think he'd be ashamed to have allowed the builders to leave it like this.'

22

My wife's indignation became embarrassing as the truth filtered through. The *devis* began to haunt me like Marley's ghost as the painful realisation emerged. I recalled vividly what I had signed to – 'not to have the rubble removed from the site'. I even remembered the architect asking me if I was sure this was what I wanted. It stung to remember I had resolutely insisted. What I hadn't understood was that it would be left on site where it fell. It would include not only the splendid chalk stone, but tiles, blocks, clay and rotten timber. In fact, there was also a great pile of white shale, surplus to requirements, but that was insignificant compared with all the other mess.

It seemed I had only myself to blame. If only I had taken more heed of his searching question and rueful smile when the rubble was first mooted. I swallowed hard and decided the best policy was to come clean to my lady about what I now understood to have been a gross error on my part.

There was a pause following my revelation, but she was wise enough to say little, while shrugging more eloquently than words could express.

'You can't clear all that by yourself,' was all she said.

Oh, but couldn't I? I wonder how many chaps will recognise the feelings of hurt pride demanding a rectifying monumental effort. It was imperative to show everyone that I was not to be crushed by this setback. I was going to make sure the builder, the architect, and all the people in the village who had witnessed this desecration and who were, even now, gossiping about it, would marvel at my nonchalance. I say, 'my' because I was not sure how far I could rely on my wife's support in this. Well, to be honest, I did know exactly how far, but refused to think about it.

It's a funny thing but, when you are confronted by your own folly, you tend to rush to protect self-image with instant action. This was one of those moments. Also something perverse was looking for a punishing endurance test; a miserable attempt to get right with myself.

I do not know if I am alone in this, but I actually hoped the endurance test would really hurt. I even began to suffer paranoia. I suspected the builder of having vindictively left the rubble for not having been allowed to take it away as part of the deal, so he could sell it on at a profit. I imagined him snarling through gritted teeth, '*Mais, oui, Monsieur*, you want me to leave you the rubble. *Bien sûr!* I will leave you it all! You are welcome to it. I drop you it, *avec plaisir*, ma frahnd!'

The nextdoor neighbour, of whom we had so far seen neither hair nor hide, was obviously peering at us from behind her lace curtains. We had heard that her son had wanted to buy the house, but I had bought before he got his finances together. I had foiled him by paying the asking price. She must, of course, be smiling her satisfied smile to think of the disaster befalling these invaders. Good heavens, the whole village had been waiting with glee for us to come and discover the scene of havoc! This was payback time for all the atrocities committed by the Black Prince! Did I hear laughter coming from the local bar below?

By the following morning, after a good night's sleep and after I had dreamed most of my fantasies out of me, I began to adopt a more rational view of the action to be taken. We sat quietly over our breakfast of croissants and coffee and looked the future in the face. We remembered that we had invited my wife's cousin and her daughter down in the summer, only two and a half months off. We had painted an idyllic picture of the place, and now all we had to offer was this scarred battlefield and a house without even basic facilities, hidden behind a forest of triffids. Sleeves would really have to be rolled up. Well so be it! It would be Agincourt again! I would throw myself 'into the breach once more', and although alone, without the 'band of brothers' to 'summon up the blood and stiffen the sinews', good old Henry V spoke clearly in my ear:

> … yet all shall not be forgot
> But we'll remember with advantages
> What feats he did that day …

24

And good old Winston Churchill stood before me in a vision,

> Never have so many been impressed
> by so much accomplished by just one.

It was my way of surviving, something from which my wife wisely disassociated herself. I sought to do the same, honest, but for me it takes time and, with apologies to the grammarians, time was something we didn't have a lot of.

4

Attention les Vipères!

Never having had to tame an over-run garden before, I was without any of the proper tools to attempt it. The nearest I had ever come to having the slightest idea of what this might entail was looking at pictures of Victorian Surrey farmworkers, and I remembered thinking they looked a fine bunch of men and women, all hacking away at the corn and gathering in the sheaves with sickles and large rakes.

Obviously, I would need both of these tools in order to get stuck in; the first to slice through the weeds and the second to pile them up for a bonfire. Fortunately I was able to get my hands on these tools the following morning from a local farmers' supplies merchant, and straight after lunch, I was ready to throw myself against Nature's excesses. I psyched myself up for the role of agricultural labourer, and pictured myself in that recalled rural tableau. There was one distinct difference. Whereas the Victorian farmworkers wore boots, dungarees or heavy linen trousers and waistcoats over flannel shirts topped with squat brimless hats, I sported a short-sleeved little number completely open at the front, a pair of knee-length shorts, open-toed sandals and a wide-brimmed straw trilby, all of which would have provoked heavy sidelong glances and muttered comments from the sepia folk of yesteryear.

However, you had to admire the way, careless of my own safety, I honed the sickle under the now quite fierce sun. I was determined to raze that garden to the ground. It would look like a bowling green when I was finished with it. I prepared myself with excerpts from Shakespeare's *Henry V*. Everyone would 'remember with advantages what feats (I) did that day'.

Without further ceremony I began to swing at the overgrowth, and my pale English legs swayed and jerked back and forth with a staccato rhythm. I would slaughter this enemy, and many would lie dead on the battlefield that day!

'I was not angry since I came to France,' *slash* 'All the budding honours on thy crest,' *slash* 'I'll crop, to make a garland,' *swipe* 'for thy head. My voice is in my sword,' *slash* 'thou bloodier villain than words can give thee out!' *slash!*

I was about to start on Henry's speech at Harfleur, when a piercing scream rent the air. No, it was not my lady protesting at my *folie de grandeur*; it came from the garden gate. I adopted the stance of a garden statue as I vaguely made out, through the tall grasses, a short female figure standing the other side of entrance. She was elderly, and was jumping up and down and waving her arms about agitatedly. She described wide arcs with one hand, while patting her sun-hat down on her head with the other. Maybe she was impressed with my rendering of King Harry and was trying to get in on the show? No, her voice was too repetitive, and resembled more a Manchester United supporter offering advice to the referee on how he should absent himself.

Not having the slightest idea what she was saying, I attempted a friendly wave back. This did not seem to comfort or reassure her at all. She became even more agitated, as if she were appealing against a foul. A string of piercing shouts ended with the recognisable phrase, '*C'est incroyable!*'

It obviously called for a more active response, and I began to wade through the gigantic weeds towards her. This action did nothing to quell her verbal outpourings. It was only when I had fully emerged from the grass and walked directly to her that she finally stopped shouting. She stood panting and glaring at me, and finally gave a deep sigh, expressive of relief and impatience, and, possibly, by now, even exhaustion. Her cheeks were flushed, and she rolled her eyes to heaven, slapped her thigh and shook her head, all in one movement.

'*Bonjour, Madame*,' I said in affable vein, wondering how to calm the poor wretch. She was having none of this friendly approach. Instead, she shook her head again, and with the heavy emphasis redolent of a parent speaking to a five year old, said,

'*Les vipères, Monsieur! Attention aux vipères! Très dangereux! Comprenez?*'

'Really? Heavens! Yes, Madame, I understand. But where are they, these vipers?'

Her eyes nearly popped out of her head, and incredulously she repeated the phrase, 'Where are they? You ask where are the vipers? You ask me where they are?' Then with both arms flung to heaven, she added in a despairing tone, 'They are everywhere! *Partout, Monsieur!*' and she pointed a quivering finger in the direction of the tall grass.

'They are hiding away in the undergrowth. You must protect your limbs from them. Always you must protect your legs, or they will get you.' Obviously I did not look convinced, so she added, '*Zut alors! Bah, oui!*' in a tone implying I had contradicted her.

I was quite ready to agree with anything she said, but to tell the truth I was also fascinated by the purple hue of her face. I guessed what she really meant was, 'Any fool knows you don't offer your nether parts on a plate to satanic creatures lurking in the grass. What does this English urbanite think he's doing?'

I could immediately picture the scene down in the village bar, as she recounted her tale of folly. She looked disdainfully at my bare legs and shook her head.

'*Oh, mon dieu!*' she said, in a resigned way. I had never thought too highly of my legs, but had never had openly adverse criticism.

There she stood, the pedagogue, and I a recalcitrant fifty-something child. I instinctively adopted a penitent expression and posture, and this seemed to bring her round to a more indulgent disposition. She shrugged several times, and informed me in a

29

markedly calmer way that she had been greatly alarmed to see me risk being mortally attacked by those wicked serpents. She wondered if I were attempting suicide. How else could she understand someone entering such a lethal terrain without any heavy boots, thick trousers tucked into long socks, or leather gloves?

I expressed my regret for such embarrassing carelessness and profound gratitude for her timely intervention. Well, yes, good – but I should know the dramatic consequences of coming in contact with these hellish creatures, and the diabolic way in which they lurked in wait, expressly to sink their venomous fangs into unwary ankles. There was one case she knew of that required amputation, and another where ... phut! And here she tailed off, signifying termination with a brief horizontal wave of the hand. If I could only have seen one of her friend's swollen, discoloured ankles and heard her cries of unbearable agony, I would never walk in tall grass ever again.

Oh, if only she could know the profound respect I now felt for these creatures! Oh, how eagerly I nodded agreement! I sensed that I was finally mollifying her with my constant head shaking of the 'wiser and sadder fellow' type. Oh, how grateful I was!

She looked closely at me, and nodding back for the first time, almost, but not quite, smiled. Her voice took on quieter authority as she gently chided, 'It is fortunate for you the angels were on duty, Monsieur. But I would not rely on their intervention all the time. God is good, but he does like to see you wearing a stout pair of boots, thick trousers and long socks when you go into the long grass.'

I was ready to put it in writing that I would, from this day forward, wear the regulation garb and always stamp about and make loud noises before taking a single step into the grass.

'Always stamp about as you approach the cursed area.' She demonstrated this with a brief flamenco dance. 'And do a lot of shouting. That will strike fear into the evil cowards, and they will slink away.'

I agreed to do a lot of stomping, heedless of public reaction, to shout and bang things together in order to strike terror in the reptiles, and loom terrible in their lives. I would be their Damocles' sword.

Just then, my wife walked up the ramp from the house and emerged into the sun. Immediately, Madame turned to her and, with a transformed smile, greeted her as if she had known her all her life. Madame bent down and picked up her basket and offered it.

'I bring you these few things to welcome you to the Charente.'

My wife accepted the basket, and Madame whipped away the cloth, revealing newly picked potatoes, lettuce and baked scones. My wife thanked Madame and, hampered by limited vocabulary, made appreciative noises as she peered into the basket as if cooing into a crib. Madame laughed self-deprecatingly, refusing any gratitude for such unworthy gifts.

'It is good you have come. The house has been empty too long.'

They smiled at each other, and I was instantly marginalised.

'How kind!' (accompanied by non-stop beaming).

'Nothing of the sort!' (positively lighting up).

The moment tailed away into silence.

Madame turned and with a brief '*A la prochaine*,' made for her own gate. '*Bon courage!*' she said, holding up an admonishing finger, 'and think on!'

I was getting really good at turning on rueful smiles. As she reached her gate, she added, 'A pity about the "cowboys". They left an awful mess for you.' And she was gone.

Her sudden and unsolicited reference to the 'cowboy' builders was encouraging. She had delivered it as if she was pronouncing the opinion of the whole village. It seemed suddenly obvious that they had no wish to be judged by these jerrybuilders.

'What was all the shouting about?' asked my wife. 'I was almost afraid to come up.'

'Oh, nothing, really,' I replied nonchalantly.

'Really?' she muttered unconvincingly, with a sidelong glance.

Minutes later, she showed a rather intrusive interest as I changed into combat attire: heavy boots, thick trousers tucked into long socks, and large cow-hide gloves, before launching myself once more against Nature's excesses.

By the evening, most of the upper garden had been sickled, and I felt pretty pleased with the result. I basked in a warm, self-righteous glow at having pitted myself against the hidden evil forces of Nature with such disregard for my own safety, and emerging unscathed. As the light began to fade slowly into a rosy evening sky I rewarded myself with a large pastis and lounged under the plum tree, squinting at the results of my labour.

There was still the one remaining eyesore; a pile of useless shale left behind by the builders, heaped like a termite nest in the middle of what might now be loosely termed a lawn. Beyond the shale lay a huge limestone boulder dumped by a mechanical digger used to excavate the hole for the septic tank.

A second pastis got me thinking. A third brought the solution, and I toasted it with the last dregs. I would rake the shale flat and call it a terrace, and pile other boulders next to the huge one and make a raised flower bed. I congratulated myself that, just in time, I had prevented myself from moving those wonderful features. I outlined this wonderful solution to my wife.

'What an intoxicating effect it will have!' I murmured with a satisfied sigh.

'Rather like your intake,' she replied, studiously looking into the last rays of the disappearing sun. I was in the mood to ignore such a remark with impunity, and closed my eyes to feel the sun's dying warmth on my face.

5

Bring on the Clowns

If I had not, at that particular moment, been brushing leaves from the steps that pass our house, we would not have received the invitation. A small family group in animated conversation came round the corner, and started down towards me, making their way to the village. They were two middle-aged ladies and a young couple with arms entwined round each other.

As only the French are allowed to say these days, they were decidedly '*gai*'. We exchanged eye contact and a '*bonjour*', as they swept past, but two seconds later, the young man stopped, turned round and said, 'You're a Brit, yeah?'

Taken a little aback, I laughed. 'It's obvious, then?' and retorted, 'You'll be from the States.'

'Yeah. You can tell us a mile off,' he said, accentuating his drawl. He walked back up the two or three steps and held out his hand, saying, 'I'm Bruce, and this,' turning to his partner, 'is Germaine. We got hitched three months ago back in LA. Did the whole thing over there, and now we're about to do it the French way.'

As I wondered what the 'whole thing' might be, Germaine joined her husband and said in English so perfect I might have mistaken her for a compatriot, 'Hullo. Nice to meet you.'

'A pleasure,' I said, giving my name. 'You can't be from this part of France.'

'Yes. My parents...' indicating one of the older ladies, 'live in

Angoulême. They have the old house by the Chateau as a holiday home.'

She turned to the two ladies below and called them up.

'*Venez. Monsieur est anglais.*' They joined the young couple and we all shook hands and exchanged names. I discovered that the second lady was Germaine's aunt.

As the two elders had practically no English, we spoke French, although I was acutely aware that I was much less accomplished in their language than Germaine was in mine.

'Are you getting married in the church down there?' I asked.

'Jees, no. We did all that stuff in LA. We're here for a shindig. Nicolette here,' he added, placing an arm on his mother-in-law's shoulder, 'couldn't make it across the big pond, so we had to come here.'

Just then my wife, having heard the voices, came out of the gate, and we repeated the name-swapping rituals. No sooner had we finished them than Bruce suddenly declared in an excited voice, 'Hey! We're having it tomorrow afternoon in the *Salle des Fêtes.*'

'Having what?' asked my wife.

'The wedding breakfast,' said Germaine.

'So why don't you guys join in? Come on and let it ... hang out for a while!'

My wife and I registered wide-eyed astonishment at such informality. We had no time to reply before Bruce exclaimed, 'Great! Let's go multi-national. Right, it's settled! *Salle des Fêtes*, tomorrow at two o'clock. Everyone uses first names, so no one feels the generation gap.'

The next second, he had gathered everyone within the circumference of his arms and proceeded to usher them down the steps again, like an eager collie rounding up sheep. At the corner of the path that turns left to the village, he shouted back, 'And for heaven's sake, don't dress up. Just come as you are! On to the boulangerie for the wedding cake!' Then he pushed them all out of sight.

Considering the threadbare state of my trouser knees, the frayed shirt sleeves and the general sweat-soiled state of the rest of me, I couldn't begin to fathom what he might have meant by 'Come as you are.'

We smiled at each other, half in amusement at this idea, and half to cover our doubts about gate-crashing on this event so unprepared. As the voices of our whirlwind hosts faded away into the village, we tried to grasp the full implications of this invitation. The leaves were much easier to sweep away than the misgivings that arose in my mind.

We were foreigners, we wouldn't know anyone there, we couldn't even recall our hosts' surnames, and we were not fluent enough in the language to be able to enjoy the jolly slang and patois that would inevitably attend a French wedding breakfast. We wouldn't even be able to buy a gift before the event.

However, since we had been summoned rather than invited, and there seemed little chance of a refusal being accepted, we decided to regard it as a fateful encounter with the unknown. Anyway, what the heck! If I could buy a house on the spur of the moment, then what fears could a French 'shindig' hold?

At two o'clock the following day we turned up outside the *Salle des Fêtes*, expecting a file of guests graciously awaiting admittance. Instead we were confronted by a village square milling with muscular male activity, surrounded on the fringes by frowning, watchful females. Trestle tables were being unfolded from a van and carried with as much bustling noise as could be mustered to the accompaniment of discontented female sighs.

Standing in the centre was a stocky character with black hair, swarthy complexion and a handlebar moustache – perfect casting for a circus ringmaster in a Fellini film. He was bellowing the simplest directions to sweating minions, who echoed them, shouting them in each other's faces.

All the women were dressed to kill; the wives of the local farmers with well-scrubbed bucolic faces and flamboyant patterned dresses, those of the urbane bourgeoisie from

35

Angoulême, and cities further afield, in quiet silks and floppy-brimmed hats. They were getting impatient, and it was not long before the farmers' wives began to amplify the noise with their own insults at their menfolk's clumsy efforts. The more refined ladies restricted themselves to raising their eyes to heaven and smiling in a superior way at each other, while studiously dissociating themselves from the less inhibited behaviour of some of their kind.

'Heaven help us all if this is the best you gorillas can do! We'll be here all day at this rate!' shouted the farmers' wives, congratulating each other with nods and laughter, as they goaded their men on in their inept activity. It only involved unfolding the legs of trestle tables, carrying them into the hall and standing them up again. It was like watching Jacques Tati erecting a deck chair. It was only after several trapped fingers and bruised knuckles that the tables went inside the hall, and the guests allowed to follow.

Even inside, the pantomime continued. The ringmaster stood on the podium and was directing his minions, with frenetic arm-waves and barked orders, to place the tables in a rectangle. He pointed imperiously in all directions at once, shook his head in disbelief at the incompetence of his workforce, and then raised his eyes to heaven like a martyred saint. The farmers' women hurled insults like a Greek chorus, but he perversely took them as praise.

The sight of twenty-odd puffing and sweating farmers one minute staggering into each other, the next coming to a frozen halt, in an effort to respond to the instructions, was too much for the ladies, who were incited to such loud insults they drowned out all possibility of hearing any orders at all. However, when every table leg had been dropped on everyone's toe, each shin bruised by someone's heel, and everyone had reversed into his fellow, the tables were at last in their right places.

The men froze again, this time in amazement at their unexpected success. They fell on each other's necks, kissed each other, patted backs and shook hands in mutual congratulation. The

Master of Ceremonies took his bow, and strutted from the platform towards the exit like a toreador, with imaginary fanfares ringing in his ears. His minions shuffled after him grinning with conceited pleasure, as the women turned their backs, and huffed disdainfully.

The moment the men disappeared, the ladies swooped on the tables like the furies, to spread cloths, lay cutlery and dishes from the kitchen, and place huge vases of flowers everywhere. The transformation through this well-oiled female machinery was immediate and made nonsense of all the previous clamour and misapplied energy.

The meal, when we were all seated, comprised huge plates piled high with an amazing variety of cold meats surrounded by bowls of sauces and salads. We wondered, in our typically British way, if horse was among it, but were not disposed to ask. It was delicious anyway.

There were few niceties as everyone reached forward without formality to help themselves from the centre of the tables, speaking and laughing with their mouths crammed. I have always been impressed by the ability of the French to eat and converse at the same time, and suppose it is because they have been well practised in the art from earliest childhood.

An elderly farmer and his wife of Italian extraction were seated next to us and showed a more absorbed interest in our day-to-day life in England than I had ever experienced before. They waited so patiently, too, as I struggled to empty my mouth of food before replying to their enquiries.

Having gorged ourselves on this course, we ploughed our way through cheeses, flans and purees, once again deposited in the centre to be pushed and grabbed at like over-sized betting chips on a croupier's table. And all the while, streams of wine frothed and flowed.

Some of the men with fuller figures brazenly loosened their belts and grunted with what I mistakenly took to be with replete satisfaction, until some servers at the head of the table suddenly made amateur trumpet sounds, and three ladies entered under the weight of a huge flat dish piled high with a '*pièce montée*', or as we would recognise it, pastry balls filled with cream (*choux à la crème*), held together with caramel sauce and basted with chocolate. The father of the bride began to serve these out into small dishes.

I was on the point of declining this when my Italian farmer friend informed me that wasn't an option, because it was the 'wedding cake'. As the spoon dug into the confectionery mountain, everyone cheered to see it still standing tall. It developed into a game of draw-sticks in which the host showed himself adept, until only a sizeable gooey ruin remained.

As soon as everyone had their helping in front of them, someone cried for speeches. Bruce stood up and would have launched into one straight away, had not the persistent shouts calling for it not prevented him. Eventually, he was able to thank everyone for accepting the invitation. Some fellow shouted back that there was no need for thanks: he'd have come whether he had an invitation or not. Someone else shouted out that that was typical of the last speaker; he always turned up for a free meal. Everyone cried 'shame!' or booed and cheered.

Far from being abashed, the original heckler wanted to know if there were any other daughters thinking of getting married; he needed to make sure he got the date right. He was shouted down, and Bruce assured them he was not going to make a long speech.

Everyone cheered again. Bruce gave up and sat down with a wave. The bride's father stood and raised his glass to the couple and everyone drank and dived into the profiteroles. Contented lip smacking and hedonistic murmurs ensued, as jaws worked in unison on the festive finale. Mothers with chocolate circles round their mouths wiped the dark smudged lips of their offspring until, with deep sighs of contentment, all spoons were laid down. As if the quiet ruminations of the well-fed were oppressive to him, the ringmaster suddenly rose to his feet and scraping his chair back announced, '*La danse!*'

He ignored all shouts of protest from the women, and gave orders for the music to start. Some responsible souls attempted to push the tables to one side, but before they could do this, the Master of Ceremonies jerked back an imperious thumb, and a crocodile began to form itself behind him.

As the music blared out, he began to shuffle forward, jabbing a finger of command at anyone sitting. Soon the whole gathering had formed up behind him in one huge file and were shuffling forward like unruly kids playing trains.

The 'salsa' seemed unfamiliar to many, and they were woefully out of step. No one was spared being part of this ragged and confused millipede, except the oldest ladies, who were carefully escorted to a safe corner. Even mothers with toddlers in pushchairs were roped in, and were forced to see the heads of their tiny charges being shaken from side to side. This Lord of Misrule had an even more diabolic plan up his sleeve. In the full evil knowledge of the inevitable ensuing chaos, he proceeded to lead the dance among the tables. Anyone attempting to push them to one side was forcibly resisted by his minions, and ordered to take their place in the line.

Beginning by weaving among the tables, he suddenly ducked and took the swaying, tottering, groaning file under one table then over another, in a ridiculous obstacle course that saw the elderly left sprawling on the floor and the middle-aged, determined to show they were still capable, straddling the table tops in incredibly undignified and revealing fashion. The children loved it, the young men took pleasure in showing off their leaping powers, and the rest of us showed we could just do it.

It was a scene straight out of a Brueghel painting, and an amazing initiation into a long-held French rural tradition of marking the beginning of a couple's life together with as much folly as possible.

The dance finished with everyone collapsing in a heap of petticoats, shirt-tails and battered hats, and then struggling to their feet to crawl their way back to some kind of exhausted composure.

Obligatory dances and games followed. Most of the games were designed to humiliate, among which was a fashion parade and dress-designing competition. I was, for my sins, given a snazzy little number created from pink toilet paper. Needless to say, I did not win any plaudits.

One game in particular remains in my memory as being particularly humiliating. It was billed by the Master of Ceremonies as 'a trial of skill and courage with a long-handled axe!' Two volunteers were selected, willy-nilly, and presented as brave and willing warriors. It was obvious that they were far from willing and, from our own feelings of gratitude at not being chosen, we can say probably not very brave, either. They would show their fearlessness, he proclaimed, by taking off their shoes and socks, wearing blindfolds, and then attempting to split, with one blow, a log placed in front of them.

They were led like lambs to the slaughter, and the ritual was played out; the log was duly positioned, blindfolds were applied and the axe placed in their hands. They were aided by having the axe head placed initially on the top of the log. What was withheld from them was the fact that their best cashmere socks were then placed on the log.

We were struck by the sadistic glee of everyone present at the sight of the contestants lining up their invisible aim to cut their own footwear in half.

'*Courage, mon brave!*' everyone shouted. 'One good blow will do it! Strike hard!'

As we joined in the shouts, we thought what a fiendish betrayal of trust it was.

The deed was done, the blindfolds taken off, and cheers rang out, as the split socks were handed back to them as their reward. The victims were presented with a replacement pair of bright orange ones for the rest of the evening, just to remind them of their credulity in trusting in the good faith of their friends.

Another reminder was a sizeable gash in the parquet floor, caused by one enthusiastically misdirected blow. Occasionally, during the evening, a group of old men would gather round it, to shake their heads and shrug philosophically as if pronouncing judgement on a younger and less responsible generation, implying that they would never have done such a thing in their day.

It was late in the evening before we summoned the courage to leave. We offered our excuses to Bruce and Germaine and her parents, who reluctantly but graciously accepted them. As for the rest of the company, they regarded our excuses as incredibly lame. We were forced to run the gauntlet, subjected to jeers and jibes, as we made our way to the exit. Typically paranoid, I imagined we were letting our whole nation down by deserting the rigours of the party. We might as well have stamped on the Union Jack as show our inability to stay in the kitchen when things got hot. We waved to show we knew what 'good sports' we all were, and left with dignified exhaustion.

We could still hear the jollity carrying on in the village below us as we prepared for bed. As we pulled the covers over our heads to block out the accordion music that drowned the sound of crickets and owls, it struck me how much better the French are at playing the fool. It had all been incredibly childish from our reserved British point of view but, as we drifted off to sleep, I hoped somewhere in the back of my mind that we had earned ourselves a kind of badge of acceptance for having taken part in those irresponsible games.

We heard later that the party had gone on until noon the following day.

· 6

A Peasant Welcome

If we ever wanted to find out what was going on in rural France, we would call on our old friend, Monsieur Boisnard to tap his wisdom and be served camomile tea by his genteel wife.

He spoke from a lifetime's experience of carving a living out of the soil, with a tenacity that had never relied on subsidies. He represents the age-old self-reliance of all true peasants. He never understood how the world could owe a living to anyone not prepared to wrestle for it with his own hands. But he also insisted on the right of every man to be given opportunities.

He loved the country he was born in and took joy in working the land that surrounded him. Although he and his wife had never moved from the village, they had lived through the most traumatic changes in the history of man. They entered life as mechanisation of farming began, survived two world wars, saw the creation of atomic energy and the invasion of space, were aware, in an uncomprehending way, of the technological revolution in communications, and finally, towards the end, heard of civil war in Europe and something called an 'ozone layer' being seriously damaged. But, as Monsieur Boisnard said the last time we spoke in his garden, 'Soon, it will not matter to me. The world has deserted our generation. Anyway, look at me! Look at my hands!' He thrust them out at me. They were curled up into arthritic knots. I shrugged sympathetically, and he outfaced my pity with a chuckle.

'All this garden, those trees I planted, and that trout pool I dammed up; these hands did it all. I even made my own tools. Now look at me!' He laughed again. 'I can hardly open a bottle with them!'

With his eager roguish gaze, he showed his readiness to surrender to the unchangeable order of things. He did not share a faith with me, and had little faith in anything but the land and the predictable seasons he and his fellows obeyed. He was passionately dedicated to husbanding the soil and deeply conscious of his duty to pass on his inheritance to others.

He knew the intimate history of every tree, shrub and flower he had planted. They were his children, protected in a sacred domain against the slightest vagary of the elements. He tended them as if he would die tomorrow. He also spoke with a directness that warned you he hadn't got time to be too polite.

As witness the time we were sitting in their living room overlooking the valley. He leant over from his chair, took my elbow in his bony grip and said, 'When I first introduced myself to you, I said to myself that if you were pleasant, I would continue to visit; if not … well …' Here he drew a thin wiry arm across his body in a gesture of finality … 'then it will be, "*Bonjour*," "*Au revoir*," and nothing more.'

He looked at me fiercely and nodded to emphasise. I smiled back, and he suddenly laughed. We both knew it would not be like that.

His wife, standing by the window seemed embarrassed and attempted to temper his blunt honesty.

44

'Oh, Papi, you remember very well what you said when you came home that day!'

'Yes, of course, I remember! "They'll pass!" is what I said.'

'Oh, you are incorrigible!' she said, throwing up her hands. Then, turning to me, she added, 'What will you think of him? He said you were going to fit in very well.'

She looked down at him with an expression that pretended to find him incorrigible and betrayed deepest affection.

He promised to prune our vines for us, and, true to his word, turned up within the week. He knocked purposefully at the gate and, without formality beyond a curt '*bonjour*', demanded a stepladder, a roll of string, and a pair of scissors.

'I don't want any stupid plastic stuff. Proper string,' he emphasised.

I jumped into unquestioning obedience. It was alarming to see this eighty-year-old peasant clambering up a ladder propped against the vine-frame and, swaying precariously with his arms outstretched to gather in the branches, grasping, pulling, cutting them with his pruning knife, and flinging them aside, like some energetic anthropoid in a tropical forest.

I shouted up to ask if there was any way I could help. He leant out even further, and without looking down at me, said, gruffly, '*Non.*'

I swallowed hard, and ventured to suggest that if, perhaps, I were to pull from the other side ...?

'*Non.*' The sound of snipping and rustling continued. Counterbalancing his weight by extending a leg in one direction while reaching out in the other, he gathered in the furthest strands. I drew breath and gritted my teeth in silence.

At length I ventured, 'Perhaps if I cut the string down here you could hold on better.'

'*Non, non, non,*' he replied like a machine-gun.

I turned away, afraid to watch any more, wincing at the imagined scene of his prostrate unconscious figure at the foot of the ladder. After the longest ten minutes, I heard him descend and looked up to

45

see the task finished. He was protected by the same God who created goats, and I of little faith immediately offered coffee.

'*Non*,' he said. 'No coffee for me.' He handed the string and scissors back to me, and with the briefest shake of the hand, said, '*Voilà!*'

'It's done then?' I muttered, quite unnecessarily.

'Yes. *Bonjour.*'

He turned on his heel before I could say anything more, passed beyond the gate and was disappearing down the steps before I could reach the lane to wave him off. He could not be doing with gratitude. The job completed, he had his own work to tackle.

This same eighty-year-old whirlwind was as gentle and forbearing a guide as ever you could wish to meet when he took you round his garden. All his floral offspring were shown off with pride, even the tiniest and most humble flowers. He would give as much attention to the tiny hyacinths that peeped out as luminous specks of blue from the undergrowth of the copse as he would to the huge azaleas he grew in great pots in the driveway.

'They hide themselves away from the light. But look,' he whispered, as he drew the fallen leaves away from them, 'how they shine in shady places.'

One very hot afternoon in August, he suddenly stood up and in a momentous tone, said, 'I will take you to see my secret garden. Come!' His wife looked startled.

'Oh, Papi, you must not go there at this time of day. It is too hot!' This was a challenge to his manhood.

'She worries too much,' he protested. 'The heat is nothing.'

He took for granted we would follow, as he strode purposefully out of the garden We hurried after, and looked back to see his wife making a resigned gesture.

The heat was intense and the grass felt dry and brittle underfoot as we walked single file towards a small coppice next to the river four hundred metres away. As we approached it, a small wattle gate revealed itself. He pushed it open and ushered us into a fenced circular garden surrounding a large pool. The river passed through it via two sluice gates made of metal rods. Below us were small schools of trout swimming in and out of the dappled light created by the overhanging willows.

'My larder,' he said. 'I can come here and watch these beautiful creatures grow to maturity for my table.'

He had made this secret garden to provide food immediately after the war in 1945. He was mayor of the village at that time and, as such, had charge of repatriating German prisoners. While they were under his supervision, he put them to the task of digging out the stewpond and, as he put it, gave them the chance to repay some of the damage they had caused to his land.

As we walked back across the scorched field, he said, 'Sometimes some people come and steal the trout. They climb down the banks and get in round the fence. Mostly they are nomads on their way through. I caught them once and said to them, "Look, respect must be mutual. You respect what is mine and I will respect you. If you steal from me, you don't respect me. If you do not respect me, you do not respect yourselves, so I cannot respect you."' He shrugged philosophically. 'They listened and nodded, but I doubt it made a difference.'

We continued the conversation when we got back to the house, sitting with a cool glass of wine in the kitchen.

'It was like that with the Germans during the war. They did not respect. They took. So we could not respect them.'

He pursed his lips and shook his head slightly to qualify this.

'Well, there were Germans, and Germans, of course. Some we got on with. I had to guard the German prisoners until they were sent home. I treated them as fellow humans and we got to respect each other to some degree before they left.'

He leaned earnestly towards us as he continued, 'Well, I tell you, when they went back to Germany, they kept in touch. One year they even came back to visit us. That is a kind of victory, no?'

We nodded, conscious of agreeing with something of which we had no experience.

Each time we left to return to England Monsieur Boisnard would rather wickedly remind us that he probably wouldn't be around when we came back. But the following season there he was, tracing his invisible paths across the valley with his loping peasant gait. The first evening we watched him strolling back and forth, and bending down to tend his beloved plants under the oblique glare of the sun's rays. He was still working away when we went in for supper.

The following day, Jeannine, our neighbour came to our gate early. She came carefully down the steps, her eyes always at her feet on the steep slope. Her face, when she looked up was empty of expression, but full of foreboding.

'Monsieur Boisnard is in hospital,' she murmured without preamble. 'At last his garden has claimed him.'

'We saw him yesterday evening ...'

'He was found on the path below his house. He was there for some time before a neighbour found him this morning.' She nodded continuously to add emphasis. 'He will not come home.'

I killed the silence with a pointless question, 'But how did it happen?'

She looked at me for a second as if I was trying to catch her out in some fabrication.

'Well, the sun, of course, is hot even in the early hours.'

'Ah, he didn't realise.'

'Oh, he knew. He knew very well.' She nodded slowly and wisely to emphasise the inference.

'But he can't have ...?'

Jeannine grimaced a clear negative. 'If he had wanted to live he should have given up his work. I say no more than that.' Everyone knew work was imperative for him.

'Ah, well,' she sighed, 'what comes to all has come to Monsieur B.'

She walked back to her gate with her rustic acceptance of life's finality. The stroke had taken Monsieur Boisnard's speech and most of his ability to move, and in those conditions he would not have countenanced going on. Madame Boisnard was taken that day to their daughter's home in Saintes. She never saw her husband again.

The sky seemed a shade darker and pressed us into numbness. I wondered if his simple respect for his fellows and the countryside he bequeathed them would tug at their minds and hearts, and remind them not to be so careless with their heritage.

We heard later that Madame Boisnard had followed her husband within two months. We felt a kind of gratitude.

7

Generation Gap

The year was taken up with moving back and forth as often as earning a living permitted. We got to know several of the village members, and this was made easier by having a reputation for being 'good eggs' at a wedding breakfast. The Italian farmer and his wife became good friends of ours, and gave us indispensable advice about such things as where to get logs for the fire, what to do about moles in the garden, and how to build fences.

I was in England, and preparing to make a final autumn trip for the year. My wife, having recovered from 'the heartache, and the thousand natural shocks that flesh was heir to' during the spring and summer, felt she had had her quota for that year and was ready to wave me off on this occasion.

As I was drawing up the list of things to do down at the house, the telephone rang. It was my step-brother-in-law. He understood I was about to make another trip out. I confessed such was the case. It had occurred to him that I might like another pair of hands to help with the work. I confessed such was the case, thinking, perhaps he was about to offer his services. He wondered, if such was the case, whether I might like to consider taking along his son, Peter? It would broaden his mind.

I mused for a while, which, on the telephone, always comes over as a pregnant pause.

Of course, he would understand if I did not have room or, maybe already had company. I confessed that such was the case.

51

Ah, right! Yes, well, but, it would be very good for him. He was a very willing worker, could roll up his sleeves, muck in, and turn his hand to just about anything: sweeping up, for example, creosoting the fences or chopping firewood. It hardly sounded mind-broadening to me, but he was very keen to sell the idea.

As he spoke, I tried to imagine the human chemistry with my fifty-odd-year-old friend who was already joining me. He was a conservative-minded intellectual TV producer, and putting him in proximity with a sixteen-year-old post-modern follower of amplified popular culture, whose father had been, for a number of years, a mechanic in Formula One racing, did not seem a strikingly good mix.

But, what the heck! I thought. We might learn something about bridging the generation gap. So I agreed.

My motives for inviting my good friend, Alistair, were entirely altruistic. As I saw it, he needed to get away from things and recover his balance after a rather messy affair of the heart. Anyone who has been in that position will know that the worst thing to follow such emotional stress is chronic inactivity. I felt sure he had been guided to me in the nick of time.

At first, he seemed to need convincing that coming away to stay in a caravan, next to a dilapidated house with minimal domestic facilities, in the middle of nowhere, for the purpose of immersing himself in manual labour, was the best thing for him. It required a great deal of persuasion to convince him that physical exertion was not only an attractive health-giving activity, but would prevent things preying on his mind.

A few 'yes, buts' later I adopted another tactic. With just a hint of pathos in the voice, I referred to the loneliness of working down there. I mentioned the invigorating air, warm autumn sunshine, good food and excellent inexpensive wine, and finished quite adroitly, I think, by saying that even these good things of life have no savour when you are alone. His better feelings left him no option, and he capitulated.

A week later we were, all three, assembled at the caravan, ready for the adventure of giving the house a face-lift, and bringing two generations into closer kinship.

Alistair has a cultured love of music and a dry sense of humour, easily shared by those who recognise his generosity behind the laconic wit. He does not suffer fools lightly. He often points fun at himself, but is not disposed to allow others, especially the young, to take that role on his behalf.

He had come to the Charente in order to find release from emotional stress, and he had his own ideas of how it might be achieved. He had accepted the benefit of immersing himself in work, but I had not appreciated that this 'release' also involved off-loading a full account of his amorous escapade to a captive audience.

Most counsellors advise listening to the injured heart with a sympathetic expression and an inclined ear. With Alistair it was a question of finding the means of keeping a straight face. His delivery can be best compared to the after-dinner speeches of Gerard Hoffnung, with whom he shares many of the same vocal cadences. (For those not familiar with Hoffnung, I suggest they hunt out his famous speech about the 'Bricklayer' given at an Oxford Union Dinner.)

A passionate affair that goes wrong has been subject matter for both pathos and comedy. How we feel depends on the perspective we hold at any one time. We often say that sexual attraction plays games on us. The ancient Greeks believed in their day that 'falling in love' was a form of madness, but neither they nor we like to admit that we play games on ourselves.

Alistair's story had all the elements required to create a comedy in the tradition stretching fromn Aristophanes to Feydeau. A synopsis might have read: 'A middle-aged man chases after a dream of resurrected youth with a younger woman within the limited confines of a canal boat. He is discovered *flagrante delicto* by his long-time partner without a single cupboard big enough to climb into; *ipso facto* caught with his trousers down. Reflecting on the incident, and the possibility of it becoming widely

53

broadcast by the third injured party, the younger woman decides to call it a day with her star-struck lover of mature years, who is left to stare balefully into the waters of the canal.'

Alistair told his tale with a narrative detachment that almost belied the autobiographical content. Although it was in the first person I was aware that, as a producer, he was shaping his story in art form, and creating a six-episode television comedy series out of it.

The second stage in his emotional recovery was the healing process of manual labour. And here I am in danger of appearing a male chauvinist. There is something that ladies just do not understand. They cannot fathom the importance of 'mess' in male creative freedom. They want to have 'mess' defined, to know where it begins and ends, and thereby miss the whole point: To define it is to destroy the very freedom it attempts to establish.

Out there, mess was the proper way of life. We needed to be pioneers who had slipped the leash of such female constraints; to create outside the demands of time, and freely rediscover a childhood preoccupation with dirt. What a liberating joy to leave tools littered over the whole surface of the table before we ate our meal, huddled round the open fire, scooping food off lap, knee and floor! What a significant aid to well-being never to have to clear dishes away or wash them, before taking up our labours again!

The new free-rolling life-style was reflected in our conversation.

'What about doing some painting this morning?'

'Nah. Feel more like a bit of plastering.'

'The windows have to be varnished.'

'Yeah,' (yawn) 'but I feel a plastering mood coming on. Yup, definitely a plastering mood.'

(Youthful enthusiasm.) 'What d'you say to a bit of music?'

(Eyes to heaven.) '*Mon dieu!* What sort?'

'The sort that gets you going.'

'To the toilet, perhaps?'

(Referee.) 'Tell you what. Let's do it tomorrow and go on a picnic.'

(Chorus.) 'Right!'

At the end of the day, more important decisions were made.

'What's the programme for tonight?'

'Better do the washing up.'

'Nonsense!'

(Well-modulated voice of cultured authority.) 'I've brought down this splendid quiz game to test our knowledge of classical music.'

(Young, brash, enthusiastic voice.) I've got these great cassettes of The Scuttlers and The Flashers.'

(Pointed.) 'Really? What for?'

'To listen to, of course.'

(Heavy irony.) 'Good gracious. In my game you're actually asked to identify the music.'

(Brightly naïve.) 'I don't know anything about classical music.'

(Acidic undertone.) 'Probably I guessed that from what we were subjected to in the car yesterday.'

'What's wrong with my music?'

'Difficult to form a judgement. Difficult to recognise it as music.'

(Referee.) 'Shall we start the game?'

'Splendid idea!'

(Ungracious, youthful resignation.) 'I won't know any answers, so I'll be quizmaster.'

(Referee.) 'Shall we roast the chestnuts on the fire?'

'If you must. I'm sipping my Cognac.'

(Sudden burst of enthusiasm.) 'I could test you on my music, too!'

(Sniffing the Cognac.) 'That's outside the bounds of fantasy.'

(Referee.) 'We don't have to do anything at all.'

(Out of the mouth of innocence.) 'We've got to wash up; there's nothing left to eat off.'

'You mean, *now*?'

'Why not?'

'Why?' (Sniffing, sipping, relishing, silence).

It was a carefree life. There was never any difficulty about allocating household duties; we simply ignored them. Cooking, however, was one responsibility that Alistair and I did take upon ourselves. Peter came from a home where red meat, two veg and chips constituted the order of the day, so could take little part in culinary art. Peter was impressed by our expertise on the double-burner camping gas stove, and invariably complimented us on the delicious gravy.

'*Sauce*, my boy. Not *gravy*. Sauce, subtly seasoned with wine and herbs.'

'Righto.'

'Look, you just keep cutting the logs, and sweep a space to eat, while we slave over the hot stove in the interests of your education.'

Peter had an innate suspicion of any meat that was not taken from a four-footed beast. Although he had eaten chicken on a couple of occasions, he obdurately resisted any suggestion of turkey. Alistair and I looked at each other and nodded sympathetically.

'So no turkey, then, Peter. Is that right?'

'Definitely. Urgh!'

'Right. No problem.'

We bought turkey breasts, cooked them in wine and herbs, called it 'chicken', and accepted his compliments.

'Cor, not bad, that!'

We asked, *en passant*, what other kinds of food he could not contemplate: we wanted to be sure he always ate what he liked. We made a list of his pet hates and cooked them all at the first opportunity, using every device to disguise them with whisks, graters and mixers. Every dish was different, like something out of The Arabian Nights, and all with the aim of introducing him to the life of the *bon viveur*.

It was not until the very last night that we shared with him the secret of this educational exercise. Alistair was cruelly dedicated to the truth.

'So, then, Peter,' he said, with an expression of intense interest, 'let's see. I think you said you couldn't possibly eat squid, right?'

'Urgh! Gross! Turns your stomach!'

Alistair and I exchanged a look of suitable astonishment.

'Well, would you believe it?'

'It takes the biscuit.'

'What night did we have that?'

(The mouth slackening) 'You wot?'

'I don't remember any complaint. Do you?'

'Not a word.'

'Wednesday, that was, I believe.'

Peter searched our faces for signs of the joke, and swallowed hard.

'That was never …?'

'I was tremendously impressed to see you tucking it away.'

'Conquering your phobia like that.'

'When you'd made your feelings about *squid* so clear.'

The exchange continued in similar vein through the whole list of pet hates including cod roe, conger eel, and horse meat. I did think it a bit unfair to mention the last, because it was untrue. We had not gone so far as to … uhm … unless, of course, Alistair had been double bluffing.

Peter went quietly green and made a discreet exit when Alistair said that he always began to salivate whenever he looked at a conger eel on the slab. He returned a few minutes later, sat heavily into the camping chair and said, 'You knew I couldn't stomach any of that stuff.'

And Alistair, without triumph, beamed and said quietly, 'But you did. So, bravo!'

Peter preened at Alistair's first ever compliment, and began to forgive us. Alistair had the comfortable smile of the Epicurean who had opened the door to La Dolce Vita.

There was, however, one nightly occurrence that Peter did not forgive. We bedded down in the caravan, Peter at one end, and Alistair and myself at the other, bundled in our sleeping bags as if ready to be buried at sea.

It was the second night at the house, and I had drifted into slumber, only to be disturbed by the sound of thunder, surf breaking on a pebble beach and a row of flapping tents. As I surfaced to consciousness, I translated this into a hurricane storm, a steam locomotive in a tunnel, and a stable of whinnying horses.

Fully awake, I traced its source to the mound of bedclothes next to me. Alistair's snores were primeval, archetypical. As I was feeling the relief of not being engulfed by a tidal wave driven by a tornado, a plaintive cry came from the other end of the caravan, the sound of tortured enslavement down the ages.

'Oh, God! This is bloody hell! Sleep! Let me sleep!'

'Poor chap,' I thought. 'Good lord, yes, indeed, it really is a pretty awful noise!'

I was on the point of prodding Alistair and expressing my concern for our night's rest, as gently as possible of course, when I heard Peter mutter, 'First one and then the other!'

I froze at that remark. What on earth was he implying? That I was somehow implicated? Another impersonation of a ship breaking up on the rocks from Alistair drew a long subterranean moan from Peter.

'Gawd 'elp me!' he breathed.

Disturbed by the noise, but conscious of the inference that I contributed to this mayhem, I decided to 'play dead' for the moment, and take up the subject in the morning. I simulated turning over in my sleep, made smacking noises with my lips, and coughed noisily enough to invade Alistair's subconscious and induce him to turn over and give us some respite. I managed to drift off before he repeated the crime.

In the morning, we rose somewhat bleary-eyed and groped our way to the percolator and the muesli. As we lifted our noses out of the bowls, and let the caffeine surge through our veins, I enquired, airily, how everyone had slept. Peter glared.

'Hah! Don't ask!'

'Didn't you sleep well?' I persisted, pitching my voice up in friendly avuncular concern.

'I didn't sleep. Period.'

'Why ever not?' I asked.

'How could anyone hope to get a wink with you two snoring your heads off?'

'Nonsense!' retorted Alistair. 'I never snore.'

I coughed before Peter could reply.

'How would you know, if you were asleep at the time?' I interjected.

'I was not snoring,' insisted Alistair.

'I'm afraid you were,' I said. 'You could feel the tremors. It has to be pretty loud to wake me, but it certainly did, I can tell you.'

Peter's eyes widened with disbelief, and then narrowed again as he let out something akin to a sardonic laugh.

'To wake *you*?' he snarled. 'There's nothing to choose between the pair of you!'

'You're telling me I snore, now, are you?' I said, defensively.

'Don't believe me?' he returned huffily. 'Ask them down in the village.'

I thought this rather rude, but kept my peace.

'Look!' pleaded Peter, 'Can't I sleep in the house tonight?'

'You can't sleep there! It's absolutely filthy!'

'Well, I don't get any sleep in the bloomin' caravan, that's for sure,' he retorted aggressively. 'I once saw this film,' he continued, with quite unnecessary hyperbole, 'where these two huge sea-lions were fighting on a beach, and last night ...'

'All right,' Alistair threw in tetchily. 'You've made your point. No need to embroider.'

'Right. So I can sleep on the floor by the fire? A tiny corner, anywhere. I won't be a nuisance to anyone.'

'It's your funeral if you catch your death.'

'I'm trying to stay alive, but at least I could die in peace.'

To tell the truth, I had lost self-esteem in this episode, and had no wish to pursue it further. I shuddered at the thought of having my snores compared with the primeval sounds that had assaulted my ears.

I gave Peter a truckle bed in front of the fire that night. He was a new young fellow from then on, working with a spring in his heels and, rather unfortunately for Alistair, a jollier whistle on his lips.

8

Beware! Artists at Work

It's quite remarkable how many people like to dress up for DIY as if a costume makes them seem seriously committed. Still, it takes all sorts, as they say.

To Alistair, flair was much more important than strenuous effort in the artistry he brought to his work, and a smart pair of overalls was an essential part of the image he needed to play his role well. He was so serious in his intentions to do a classy renovating job in the house, that he bought himself a lovely blue one-piece overall at the French supermarket, with zip front and matching twin outside breast pockets that you could stuff paintbrushes in when you were up a ladder. He said that blue was good, because it gave a typically Gallic look to his performance.

Peter and I looked him over and duly admired the outfit. I said it was certainly good enough to fool anyone outside France, which pleased him. I was happy to wear 'oldies' that had seen better days. I felt that the well-worn look seemed to express a more experienced approach to the work. None of the workmen I ever employed had come to work in spanking new outfits. I bought a fine pair of overalls once, and never wore them for fear of getting them dirty.

I was a bit forthright with Alistair at the beginning, and told him I wasn't sure that his overalls didn't smack of the amateur. I didn't understand how you could feel free to do a good job when you were always worried about getting them dirty or even ripped.

He pointed out that every dirty or ripped pair of overalls had started out pristine, and that he had no intention of worrying what happened to his, one way or the other. In any case, he said he didn't like looking down-at-heel, even if he were doing the manual tasks.

Once we got started on the work, we showed ourselves to be incredibly inventive. None of us had any training and we had learned any do-it-yourself skills by doing it ourselves. It was trial and error that eventually led to trial and success.

Alistair's flair was not only in the expert handling of trowel and brush that he developed, it lay also in the way he inspired us with his visionary approach. He flourished his paintbrushes with a panache reminiscent of Cyrano de Bergerac, as he studied the walls he was about to paint. He eyed the surface as seriously as Leonardo da Vinci would have done.

Each wall was a canvas to Alistair, and he had to size it up for a long time before the vision matured and became real for him. I did wonder if quite so much contemplation of the work was strictly necessary, but he puffed on his cigar and assured me that he was in the middle of an important gestation period.

Peter interrupted at one stage to tell us that on the street where he lived, we'd both have been beaten up for behaving like a pair of bozos. He said that while we had been looking at the work, he'd done a lot of chopping, and slapping of varnish on the doors, without any contemplating or anything. We just accepted that this was the result of immaturity on his part; being young, he could not appreciate the artist's need to fine-tune himself before proceeding to action.

But when the mind had prepared itself, we worked as a remarkable team. While I sawed wood to make dry-wall frames, Alistair painted the beams and Peter, with a kerchief over his nose like a Wild West bank robber, treated the doors and windows with insecticide. This is pretty strong stuff, and must not be inhaled. It has to be strong because the worms can do serious damage out there.

There are two kinds of insect, both of which bury their larvae in the wood. Much the worse is the Capricorn bug, which can munch huge holes in the fabric of a house, especially if made of pine or other soft wood. It attacks oak, but usually only eats its way along the outside of the beams, leaving the centre untouched.

There were clear signs of the main oak beams in the house having been eaten, but they must be at least four hundred years old and hard as iron. They are stronger than ever now, and any Capricorn that tried its mandibles on these would need serious dentistry afterwards.

In the case of the late unlamented haven for arachnids, the roof had been virtually gnawed to finger thickness. In a very short time it would have fallen of its own accord, if the builders had not pulled it down. So treating all the visible wood is the first job anyone should tackle out there; the region is susceptible to serious attack.

I was concentrating on changing the layout of the whole living area, and proposed to do this with dry-wall partitioning, called *cloison* in France. This is constructed of a sawn wood framework covered with plasterboard and the space between filled with glass wool for heat retention and noise suppression. This has the added advantage of permitting all the electric wiring to be hidden away inside the wall at the same time. Switches are easily attached to the wall, so long as you design the framework to include wooden backing for these before you put the plasterboard in place. When complete these *cloisons* had to be knitted into the existing stone walls with a mix of finishing plaster.

I aimed to do this at the same time as I made good the window surrounds where the wall had been cut out. I had done some amateur plaster rendering in England, and had been pleased to find that brick walls absorb the moisture in the lime mix and quite naturally pull it on to the surface. Plastering on stone, however, is much more difficult, and it requires the surface to be thoroughly wetted before sloshing the plaster on.

I discovered it was made easer if I gouged out some of the joints between the stones to give the plaster a deeper key. This is not generally difficult to do in old stone Charentais houses, for here plaster is mainly composed of hard clay, more friable than modern mortar and therefore much better suited to the effect of settling that occurs over the ages.

We were a disparate team, each working within his parameter, yet all dedicated to the same aim of creating a habitable space. Each was blithely absorbed in his allotted task, to the mixed accompaniment of Rachmaninov's Third Symphony and the whistled strains of the Mersey Beat. A cruising rhythm took over as we blocked out each other's world. In periods of relative quiet, only the swishing appropriated it, as if a percussionist had been given a long passage to brush the drum skins.

Whenever we stopped for 'brew', as Peter insisted on calling it, (that, apparently, being the name real workers used) I took photographs of the progress, which, I had to admit, was considerable. Alistair, having been totally engrossed in his work, would become in an instant alert and focused as soon as the lens was pointed his way. Perhaps it was a professional interest that made him conscious of the camera but as soon as I turned it towards him, he leapt into character.

We have to this day a series of post-card size photographs of Alistair triumphant with raised brush, Alistair prophetic pointing with trowel, Alistair blissful conducting with intense expression, and Alistair facing front in Victorian stance with enigmatic smile. They would make a wonderful billboard advertisement for something or other. (I am not sure what. Possibly a life endowment policy.)

As soon as the photo-call and brew were finished, he returned with single mind to the task in hand. He was soon into painting the walls with white emulsion, and so involved in this that he did not realise he was fast covering not only the walls but his lovely blue overalls. His cavalier brush strokes were gradually making him fade into the background.

I speculated that, if he continued to splatter himself at the same rate, he would fairly soon disappear altogether. He already had Mickey Mouse white hands, his hair made him look like a prematurely white sage, and his shoes had a two-tone mottled snakeskin look about them. Even the ladder he stood on was fast disappearing.

This seemed to him a small price to pay for the vision he aimed to realise. Gone were the streaked sky-blue walls broken up with battleship grey rectangles where the wardrobes had stood of old. Now the pristine and pure minimalist white shone with hope. But now that everything was virginal white, the jagged edges and grey stone stood out worse than ever.

As I nailed the last plasterboard in place, Alistair was already making a mix of sand, cement and lime. Normally, when plastering inside, I tack two laths to the wall as guides, then spread the plaster between them and lift off the surplus with a thin length of wood gradually shifted side to side over the surface in a see-saw action. The professional probably regards this as cheating, but as an amateur I have no conscience.

Alistair had had another vision. Whereas I had it in mind to make as smooth a finish as possible, he pointed out that it would not be in keeping with the original. He was right. The original plaster had been applied freehand, in such a way as to allow the irregular shapes of the stones beneath to show through. Therefore, too smooth a finish would not blend in.

He was adamant in believing we should aim for the same undulating surface, and regarded it as his duty to retain the essential rustic character of the original plaster, which had probably been applied around a hundred to a hundred and fifty years previously. When the building had been erected, possibly well over four hundred years ago, there would have been no plaster at all, but I was not contemplating that kind of purist return to its origins.

Having seen Alistair's liberal application of the white paint, I was apprehensive about the effects that dolloping plaster would have on him and the surroundings. On the strength of his recent performance, he could be expected to finish up in a plaster mould. But what the heck! We had come here to be liberated from female sanctions, to circumvent stultifying orderliness and to create with originality and abandon.

I concentrated hard on covering over screw-holes, and made every effort to ignore the sloshing sounds made by Alistair as he flung his sloppy mixture on to the stone surrounds. It sounded like the oars of novice oarsmen slapping the waves of a choppy sea. I kept my back resolutely turned away. It was not fair to look, and would have inhibited him, and, come to think of it, me. Slop! Slurp! Flop! Flurp! came over my shoulder with unnerving regularity, followed by intervals of barely perceptible scrapings and pregnant silences. I tensed every muscle to conserve faith in my fellow worker.

Just as I came to the end of my self-control, I heard him flick his lighter, and the smell of cigar drifted past my nostrils. He let out a satisfied sigh, which I took, with indecent haste, as a subtle invitation to inspect his handiwork.

I turned to confront the scene, and was truthfully amazed at what he had accomplished. Where I had expected a slushy snow scene, there was an iced confection that any *pâtissier* would be proud of. He had blended the new plaster with the old so well, you could not see the join.

I stared in disbelief, and Alistair smiled the smile that great artists only permit themselves when they know they have surpassed their highest standard of excellence.

Another photo-call was set up and the triumphal pose was recorded for posterity. In the resulting picture, he stands like a magician who has dazzled his audience with some incredible legerdemain.

Having captured the moment, I begged him to sacrifice status and explain how he had achieved the miracle. It was beguilingly simple, and anyone who has a similar problem to solve should pay close attention.

You simply slosh on a sloppy wet plaster mix with a trowel, to cover the whole of the area to be finished. Then you wait until the limestone sucks most of the moisture out of the mix before scraping off any high spots with an upward sweep of the trowel blade held at a forty-five-degree angle. You can then simply smooth any irregularities and slight fissures out with a wet paintbrush. If there are any really stubborn proud areas, you press harder as you brush across the surface. After that you stroke with a soft dry brush until it hardens completely. If it crazes later, you can use a fine flexible cement to disguise it all.

This was witness to the power of inductive experimentalism, a great boon arising out of gifts of time and patience, so long as you do not mind the time spent later, scraping the mixture off floor and clothes.

Such were Alistair's brave efforts that the room he helped to create is named after him to this day.

9

My Cup Runneth Over

It is a blessing to be kept in ignorance of catastrophes you can do nothing about. When I have been ignorant of problems I might have foreseen, it rather makes me want someone to kick my backside.

When people smile and nod wisely as they quote Gray's dictum, 'Where ignorance is bliss, 'tis folly to be wise,' I want to shout 'bunkum!' very loudly right down their ear. It is very silly, and potentially damaging to the psyche, to go round being philosophical, stirring up memories in the minds of those who have suffered from self-inflicted ignorance.

If only I had taken seriously my previous experiences, I might have prepared for the worst. If the Charente region is not making things grow at an indecently fast rate, or hiding beasties programmed to attack you in tall grass, it will creep up on you with dramatic climatic excesses. It was to do with the latter that I was to learn my next lesson.

I had waved Alistair and Peter off with a smile and a feeling of accomplishment. The interior of the house held not a stick of furniture, but at least looked as if it might accommodate it without covering it with dust and damp fungus. Left alone, I decided to concentrate on making something of the shower room. This was, as yet, a shell, which I had visions of transforming into a haven of bodily refreshment. A shower sounded about right, I thought, and duly set about building one.

This can sound pretty impressive to many people. Indeed, I have secured the attention of neighbouring guests at dinner parties on several occasions, and regaled them with the fascinating details. It is usually the attention of people who are happy to admit they have never held a blow torch or a spanner in their lives, and so I can be reasonably creative with the truth.

There is one group of friends in which I circulate, where most people are open mouthed at the idea of anyone other than a plumber or bricklayer even contemplating doing such a thing. I can convince many listeners that I do it for pleasure, but when taken aside later and grilled by the more sceptical men, I am forced to admit it was because I did not have the money to pay somebody else to do it.

They smile with intense relief and then nod sympathetically. I understand why of course. Later that evening as they snuggle down to sleep, they are able to discredit my story and restore their status. And why not? I would do precisely the same.

But to return to the task in hand. I was determined to have some hot water coming out of something in that shower room before I left at the end of that autumn stay. The first task was to divide the whole space into separate toilet cubicle and washing area. Now, I am ready to admit here, but not necessarily to any seated guests, that it is much easier than most people, who would never touch a trowel with a barge pole, can imagine.

In France it is made particularly easy by a product they call *carreaux de plâtre*. These are large squares of thick plaster with a protruding lip on one side and a channel on the other, which fit, one upon the other, like pieces of Lego, and are held together with a cement glue. Not only are they easily erected, but being narrow, they are space-saving. In a remarkably short time I had divided the two areas with walls that reached to the ceiling, and created the spaces for inserting doors at a later date.

I constructed the shower cubicle round the shower base, which I lay on breeze-blocks or *agglos* as they are called, with space beneath for the waste pipes. The next stage, fixing tiles to the shower cubicle walls, was accomplished without incident and, since there was no one else to do it, I heartily congratulated myself.

Picture if you will the laying of the pipes. I unpack all the lengths of copper pipe and next to them the French couplings. I address them together and discover that they do not correspond. Try as I might, it is impossible to line up half-inch tubing with fifteen-millimetre fittings, and there's an end on't. I drop everything, dispense with all the English copper pipe, and rush off to the nearest supermarket builders' merchant.

A dark-skinned gentleman with inscrutable eyes shows me his twelve-millimetre copper tube, which he tells me is standard size for most household appliances. He avoids looking at me, as if he finds my Caucasian colouring difficult to trust. I remember my propensity for paranoia, and put it to the back of my mind. He directs me to 'fixtures and fittings' in the plumbing section, and pointing vaguely towards a bewildering collection of 'elbows', 'straights' and 'tee-shaped' connections, turns on his heel and leaves me to use my imagination.

Now there are two kinds of imagination possible here; one a reasonable expectation of success, based on practical experience, and the other, which flies off into fantasy fuelled by one's vision. The first demands a 'hands-on' approach to a problem, the second a blind faith in a dream.

Naturally, I choose the second, as being something I know and trust, and more compatible with my temperament.

Since I can buy everything on a 'use or return' basis, I grab whole handfuls of every kind of fitting that looks as if it might be even vaguely useful, and take them all back to my artisan's den. There it lies, all this shining copper in various forms, ranged on the floor like an exhibition at Tate Modern.

I scrabble about with the packages, admiring their shapes like a child at Christmas with a construction set. As I do so, I am intrigued to see variously written on them, the words '*huit-dix*', '*dix-douze*', and '*douze-quatorze*'.

I turn to the lengths of pipe and see, next to the price bar code, a small ticket which says '*dix-douze*'. It does not take too long, even for me, to work out that there is an intended correlation here. As far as I know, I have been given twelve-millimetre pipe, and now discover it is 'ten-twelve'. Attempting to fit them together loosely – or 'fixing them dry', as we seasoned workers in the trade say – it is obvious that many are the wrong size.

Back I drive to the enigmatic gentleman with the dark heavy-lidded eyes to tell him I seem to have taken the wrong fittings. He looks at them as if he is going to hypnotise them, and says with great confidence, and maybe a little annoyance, '*Bah, oui!*'

He sweeps all the pieces together, ticks them off and gives me a credit note.

The more I negotiate with the Charentais inhabitants, the more I come to learn that the interjection '*Bah, oui*' is a stock response, mostly accompanied by a deep shoulder shrug, a splaying of the arms, and a mouth shaped like an inverted melon slice. This is to suggest that 'Yes, indeed, that is so, and only a completely incompetent person could have made such a ridiculous blunder, right?'

'Ten-twelve' I now discover, registers both the inside and outside diameters of the pipe. For parts to be connected they must all correspond to it. I return a large number of *huit-dixs* and *douze-quatorzes*, and numbers begin to trip off the tongue and become embedded in my subconscious.

Another thing to give me some grief is the fact that the French don't have 'Yorkshire' fittings. You can imagine how that goes down when I complain about it to that dinner guest. I am in full flow, and throw out, 'The difficulty is, they don't sell Yorkshire fittings over there.'

'Really? How interesting!' (pause) 'What have they got against Yorkshire?'

'Um, er, no, they're not being chauvinist. It's just that their connections don't have rings of solder inside them, you know, to make it flow more easily inside the joint …'

(Extended pause.) 'Really? How interesting!'

'Yes.' (Long pause.)

'Yes. Would you mind passing the tartare sauce, please?'

Nobody seems to understand how much I missed the 'Yorkshire' in my pipes, however emphatically I express it. Not wishing to sound boringly technical, I explain in a tone of deep concern that having no Yorkshire fittings means I am forced to smear flux in the joints, and lay the coil of solder on the joint in one hand while playing the blowlamp on it with the other.

'If the solder does not completely fill the space between the pipe and fitting, it will not be watertight,' I go on to insist.

'The side salad, if you wouldn't mind.'

'Any plumber worth his name finds it child's play. With me it takes ages.'

'Surely not. And the vinaigrette.'

Another problem to be overcome was that of getting electricity to a water heater, especially since the wires had not yet been laid to all parts of the house. It came to me in a flash that the quickest way to get round this was to install an instant gas water heater. I could simply screw it onto the wall and connect it to the mains and the shower taps. The gas container would be stored in a cupboard beneath it.

It only took me five times longer than a professional to complete this project, but it ended up all soldered to watertight perfection, and ready to go. The layout of the pipework possibly resembled the approach to Waterloo station, but at least the water flowed without leaking a drop. Hallelujah!

None of the dinner guests I have met has truly understood the elation that wells up on seeing hot water come from a tap that one has installed oneself. I almost pity the professional, who can expect his plumbing to work simply because it always has. For me as an amateur, it is a moment of blissful self-affirmation.

At that moment, like the insanely in-love Tevye in Fiddler On The Roof, I danced round the shower room, stripped all my clothes off with abandon and skipped under the warm stream. It was, indeed, a 'miracle of miracles'!

I was now able to leave the house in the certain knowledge that on our return in the spring, my beloved other half would be transported by the sheer luxury of it all. Turning off the mains, turning on the alarm, and firmly closing the door, I drove back to England, suffused with the sweet, warm smell of success.

What a picture I painted on my return home. What a success story! No more would she have to stand in a zinc bath, pumping water with her foot to a head-height shower ring inside a canvas loo tent.

I worked her into feverish expectation, which, despite my graphic description, she somehow managed to hide pretty well before asking where the soap dish and towel rail had been placed.

A little taken aback, I suggested that things like that were gilding the lily, whereupon she gave me a lecture on the dangers of having soap sliding everywhere, and the humiliation of having to grope around for a towel when stepping out of the shower in the 'altogether'. All these things would be added, I promised, feeling absolutely sure that she was bound to feel an irrepressible surge of gratitude as soon as she saw my handiwork.

The following April we were on our way back to the house, full of anticipation and confident that Nature was being kept in its place. We had arranged for the garden to be kept within bounds and, as we drew up at the entrance, were delighted to see the plum tree full of blossom, the vines pruned back and clusters of cowslips dotted here and there. We walked confidently down the ramp, brushed free of leaves, and, peeping through the glass panes of the door, saw the late afternoon sun reflected through all those wonderful new windows.

Once inside, having cherished the cleanliness of everything (more precisely, the space), I began to behave like an eager bell-boy at the Savoy, guiding my wife discreetly towards the *pièce de resistance* in the shower room.

At last we stood before it. This was where we would refresh

ourselves and be suffused with the after-glow and bonhomie that only the outpourings of warm water can provide. I would, I said pointing dramatically to the door, forthwith and with all haste withal, turn on the mains and she would see the miracle for what it was.

I climbed to the top of the ramp and turned the mains faucet on.

Immediately a loud screeching came from the house, which I might have taken to be a sound of transporting delight had it not been followed by the exit of my drenched wife, blinking and wiping drops of water from her face.

'Turn it off!' she shouted. 'It's pouring out of everywhere!'

I obeyed her command and, with a horrified sinking feeling, went back to the shower. Yes, no doubt about it. Water was everywhere, and where it had not spurted from holes it had spouted from pipes that had been untimely ripped from each other – not only in the shower room, but also up in the loft, where I had laid the pipes from the kitchen. There was water just about everywhere.

The brain clicked once more into that painful mode of tracking down the cause. It did not make excessive demands on the intellect to deduce what it was. A deep frost had done its worst.

The following morning I had a word with a friend in the village, who happened to be a plumber-cum-electrician-cum garden-tamer, and in the short exchange learned that January had been one of the coldest for years. Apparently the Charente had been visited by '*La lune rousse*' or 'Red Moon', and pipes had been bursting all over the place.

It was fortunate I had turned the water off at the main when I left in the autumn, or who knows what would have happened? However I had neglected to completely empty all the pipes as well. Not only had they all been forced apart but the inside of the gas heater had been completely distorted, and was now *foutu* or rendered inoperable, to put it nicely.

With not only the pipes but also my bubble well and truly burst, it took less than five minutes for my French neighbour to convince me that I needed an electric system with a fibre-lagged, thermostatically controlled water cistern – which he would help me install (here a French-style shrug) if I would like him to, of course.

I invited him to discuss it that night after work, over a glass of red wine.

'*Pourquoi pas?*' he said.

'*Pourquoi pas.*' I echoed. And so we did.

10

A Shocking Incident

The wine has been opened. My plumber friend and I sit opposite each other. We exchange pleasantries about weather, the cost of living, and how we could put the world right in five minutes.

Pierre has thick black curly hair, sallow skin, and a beard slightly longer than the 'designer' kind, suggesting neglect rather than image. He is about five feet eight, very stocky with broad shoulders and he carries himself with a careless air that declares, 'Don't mess with me.'

We got to know him and his wife Danielle through their two young daughters. They lived directly below us in the village, and we had a vantage point over their small courtyard in the main street. From the moment we started working in the garden, they waved to us and shouted, '*coo coo!*' At first it was with timid reserve, but encouraged by our returned waves, they were soon gesticulating like marooned sailors to a passing ship.

Two or three days later their mother joined them and waved over the children's bouncing forms. The next stage was an exchange in the village on my way to the *boulangerie*, and finally, after two further weeks of energetic semaphore exchanges, we invited them all, Pierre, Danielle and the two girls, up for an *aperitif.*

From there it was easy to come to an arrangement about the surveillance of the house and the maintenance of the garden in our absence. This was agreed on a friendly basis; that is to say, one friend would wish to recompense the other for his neighbourly act. In fact, Pierre made it very clear that he would only do it for a friend.

We were grateful and pleased to be thought of as such, and it was with this taken for granted that I now thought it possible to suggest that, for a fee, he might help me to install an electric water heater, known in France as a *chauff-eau*.

'*Bah, oui! Pourquoi pas!*'

'*Parfait!*'

'But, I weel only do thees as a friend.'

'That's splendid. But I must pay you for your help.'

'That ees OK but, only as a friend.'

He reached over the table and we held hands as if about to arm wrestle, then sipped more wine and nodded quietly and reflectively; a silent celebration to the excellence that comes from friendship.

I asked, casually, with a slight shrug of the shoulders and dismissive gesture of the hand, how much he thought it would cost.

'Bah, a very leetle price.'

'Well, yes, but apart from the cost of the *chauffe-eau* and connections, how long will it take, and what is your hourly rate?'

'*Bah, non!*' He appears affronted. 'It is not necessary to count the hours.'

'OK,' I pause to find a way to rephrase it. 'Then how much do I pay you for your help?'

'You do not pay me. Eet ees for an *ami*, no?'

'But we agreed. It is only right.'

'*Bah oui!* Of course!'

'So give me some idea.'

'Thees ees not possible.'

He gives a deep shrug of the shoulders and appeals to my sense of decency, and his head shakes all responsibility back into my half of the court.

'You are a friend,' he adds, as if that explains everything.

I feel as if part of the plot is lost to me. Right. So I am a friend. That has been well established, and is not an issue. When it comes to paying him for his help, we move into mystical territory.

'So,' I attempt with some delicacy, 'I must pay you, but I need to know how we can work out the amount, yes?'

He takes immediate exception to the word.

'*Non, pas du tout!* There is no amount.' He curls his lip in scorn at the last word. He nods and opens his eyes wide to provide encouragement. 'You geev mee wat you want. A gift.'

'It would help me if you put down on paper how much you charge for each hour of work.'

'*Bah, non!* Then you do not geev me as a friend. I am sateesfied wiz wat a friend wants to geev me.'

I falter like a chess player unsure of his next move.

'Suppose I say … I mean, if I were to suggest … just as an idea, you understand, and not that I know what the right amount should be … we-e-ell … er, u-hm' (taking the plunge) 'x number of francs.' I tail off, wincing internally and try to look casual.

'Eef that ees what you theenk eet ess worth,' he shrugs vaguely, 'then x number of francs ees wat you geev.'

'We-e-ell, I don't want you to think it is what I think it's worth …'

This continued between deep gulps of wine, as if two school kids were swapping comics and cigarette cards. In the end I settled on a figure that elicited minimal response, and hoped it meant he was satisfied with that 'amount'.

The big bonus was that he was immediately available, and could do it the following day. I was to serve as his apprentice assistant, and was expected to support the weight of the heater as Pierre screwed it onto the wall, feed wires through holes he had made so he could connect them up for power, and generally hand him tools like a nurse to a surgeon.

Together we took no more than three hours to complete the job. The water heater was positioned, the pipes connected and the electricity all wired up, and by lunch time, after a final celebratory glass of wine, we were able to wave him off. Everyone was contented, he with his payment and I with the work.

Now for the dedication of the whole project to my wife, and like a knight offering a gift to the lady of his choice, I invited her to take the initiatory shower.

I lit a roaring log fire in the old chimney of the house for her to warm herself as she dried her hair, and while she was to enjoy the luxury of it all, I sat in a camp chair to read a book. The fire crackled in a satisfying way, the lady hummed *sotto voce* as she prepared to enter the holy of holies. There was the rewarding sound of sprayed water, and I basked in the joy of accomplishment.

The next moment there was a scream like the shrillest ever perpetrated in a Hammer horror film. The book jumped out of my hand of its own accord, and I rose as if propelled from beneath by a rocket. Before I could reach the shower room, I was met by a very distraught lady wrapped in a towel, stabbing her finger towards the shower and hurling unintelligible curses at it. She had left the taps gushing out their precious steaming water, and I rushed to turn them off.

Following her into the living room, I found her crouched and shivering, half in tears and half in purple rage. I held her to instil calm into the situation, having no idea of the cause of this outburst. I feel sure that it is in times of stress and the heat of the moment that we choose the wrong words. This was probably one of those occasions.

'What is it, my sweet?' I asked. 'What on earth's caused the dramatics?'

I knew it was the wrong phrase the moment it passed my lips.

'Dramatics? Is that what you think?' She wiped away the tears of anger with the towel, and sat in the chair to gather herself.

'All I meant, was that the sound coming from ...'

'You'd have been dramatic if it'd happened to you! It was horrific!'

I kept my voice calm and my choice of words circumspect.

'Well, my dove, that's what I'm trying to establish. What did happen?'

I have never been able to fathom precisely what it is about a man's attempt to pacify a woman that so infuriates her. Is it that the more a man tries to obtain information from a woman to help him make sense of what she is undergoing, the more she takes that as proof that he is incapable of understanding anyway.

'*Happen?* You think it just *happened?* It was *dreadful!*'

'I'm sure it was. I mean, it must have been.'

'Not must have been! It was!'

'I believe you. I really believe you. I would just like to know what I am believing.'

'You don't believe! You'll just laugh, knowing you.'

'I promise I won't laugh. Honestly. Just tell me what happened.'

'The shower flex is alive. It attacked me.'

I laughed. My wife looked daggers. I stopped laughing. I stammered out my apology.

'Look, I'm sorry. Unforgivable. It just sounds like something out of a wacky fifties, low-budget horror film.'

She looked at me as if I were guilty of betrayal.

'Well,' I added, 'you make it sound as if the flex had a wicked will of its own.'

She stared back at me with grim determination.

'It wrapped itself around my neck and stung me. I had to fight it off. How would you explain it?'

I could not. I decided to inspect the showerhead for myself.

It was pure fantasy, I told myself as I approached the cubicle, yet treating the exercise with more respect than I could find rational cause for. I rolled up my sleeves, reached in and lifted the shower head off the tray, where my wife had dropped it. It looked passive enough. I held it in one hand and, turning the rose away, opened the hot water tap. A wonderful, forceful spray shot out of the head, and at the same time a forceful pain shot up my arm and round my shoulder. I yelped and released my grip on the hose.

To my horror, the hose did not release its grip on me, but wrapped itself lovingly round my arm. I shook it off with a violence that I did not have to consciously think about. It lay in the tray spitting its lethal poison at me. I turned and fled.

Something flashed across my mind, and I obeyed an instinct to turn off the electricity at the mains. This done, I turned back to my wife, who was standing triumphantly in front of the fire with a defiant and unsympathetic expression.

'So?'

'You're right,' I nodded, my mouth crammed with humble pie. 'It's crazy, but the whole thing's alive. Maybe we'll get water coming out of the light switch next time we turn it on.'

'I don't think we can joke about it.'

'I'm not. There's something wrong somewhere.'

'You don't need to be a genius to come to that conclusion.'

She had now recovered, and was able to address the problem in calm irony.

'If it hadn't happened to you, you wouldn't have believed me, would you?'

I had to see her point of view.

'Probably not,' I said with as much remorse as I could muster.

'What do we do next?'

'I'll get Pierre to come and look at it tomorrow.'

Pierre arrived. I had tried to describe the problem over the phone, and had failed miserably. He obviously thought I was having difficulty with the language and with a brusque 'Tell me tonight,' put the receiver down.

Another bottle was opened, and I related the incident to him as he sipped his glass and listened passively. I was disappointed that he didn't open his eyes in astonishment, or say a single *'Bah, ce n'est pas possible!'*

He listened far too patiently for my taste. When I had finished he smiled and said, 'There is a solution to every problem. I will go and see for myself.'

I turned on the main switch, accompanied him to the shower

and stood back at a safe distance. He turned the taps on with great confidence and then, with another superior smile, reached out to grasp the hose.

The yelp, when it came, was curiously satisfying. I viewed his wrestle with the silver metal snake with an equanimity that I found unusual in myself.

When he had shaken himself free and cursed sufficiently, he went back to the living room, and frowned suspiciously as he nursed his hand. With a last look of thunder, he suddenly strode to the switchbox and probed among the wires with his screwdriver. A quick inspection elicited a triumphant shout.

'V*oilà!* There is the problem,' he bellowed. '*Simple!* The heater is not connected to the earth!'

I shook my head and, losing all sense of diplomacy, asked in a very bald way, 'And why is it not connected to the earth?'

He laughed, spread his hands out in an expansive gesture, and retorted, 'Bah, that is evident! You did not attach an earth wire.' He followed this with the unanswerable question, 'How can it be connected to the earth if you do not attach the wire? *Voilà!*'

There was no point in responding to the unanswerable, so I bit my tongue. However, he was not content to leave it there, and felt it his duty to make sure I understood the importance of earthing all electrical appliances. He gave a name 'static electricity' to the problem and assured me that it was the responsibility of every householder to provide their own earth connection.

Unlike British power supply, the power in France does not come already equipped with an earth. When this fact is ignored, a sizable build-up of static charge occurs and travels along the water-filled copper pipes with spectacular results for the unsuspecting bather.

'Ah!' I said, in a tone which attempted to simulate gratitude and acceptance of blame. 'That explains it!'

He downed the last dregs of his glass, and left with a cheery wave of self-esteem.

As soon as he had gone, my wife turned to me and said,

'Honestly, not to put in an earth wire! You might have been responsible for seeing me off.'

I expressed my sense of self-righteousness with what I hoped was a look of wounded pride before replying with suitable irony, 'You're quite right. I was entirely to blame for not advising the electrician I had paid to do the job, to attach the earth wire. I apologise.'

I could not understand how, having expressed her gravest doubts about male capabilities in the electricity department, she was satisfied to leave it there. Pierre left me with an unforgettable lesson, and Mother Earth took on a new meaning.

Often after that Pierre would sit with us in our courtyard, and review the international scene. According to Pierre the French and English often pretend to like each other. He is not so easily fooled. He will tell you the cultural differences are too great, and they accept each other only because of the economic ties. He has a distinctive habit of referring to himself in the third person.

'The European Community eez made for the multi-national corporations. Wat does that mean for poor Pierre? *Hein? Rien de tout!* Nothing! It permits us to pull down the fences between your garden and mine, that is all.'

His opinions are tempered with good humour, and even his opinion that French and English are incompatible is spoken with a candour that he intends as a compliment.

In his house there is a huge picture of his village enlarged from a postcard dated 1850. This represents his roots. He wants to hand them on to his children and the picture is part of a romantic dream he carries.

At the end of the day, Pierre is himself a romantic *artiste* trapped in the body of a free-spirited plumber and electrician.

11

Assault on the Enemy

Spring gave way to summer and we now had a base from which to begin to explore the surrounding country.

In place of a primus stove, we now had a cooker and kitchen units, and, in front of the fireplace, two real chairs with cabriole legs and lightly padded arms. I was pleased that one was called a 'Voltaire', which made me feel more French when sitting in it. They were both bought from a dust-laden secondhand emporium in Angoulême. Two rugs brought over from a local Surrey market gave a modicum of homeliness to the bare oak boards, which now had a wonderful polished smell that spoke of cared-for age.

I had spent a considerable period on my hands and knees working the polish into the floor with a shoe brush, and was pleased with the lustre where no polish had ever lustred before. French polishes are wonderful and can restore wood to a wonderful condition in no time, even boards that have been interminably trodden by farmers through the ages. They come in every shade, from ash through light and ancient oak to the darkest walnut. I chose the walnut because it gave an instant ancient look.

Although we were taking some time off to discover the scenery and history of the area, we were still ticking off the jobs: the shower room had been tiled, the wash-bowl, shower and toilet were up and running, and electric cable had been laid to all parts of the house. Waiting to be done was the erection of partition walls, the insertion therein of more electric sockets, and … the unmentionable place, the thought of which brought on sweating and palpitations ... the *cave*.

We often suppress the disagreeables of life until they press their noses against the window panes of our souls. I had not merely placed this particular nightmare in the back corner of my mind, I had tried to destroy the very thought of it. Freud warned us of the dangers of repressing fear, for it will burgeon inside you and, when it emerges, will be the nightmare from Room 101.

I refer to the *cave*, the dark forbidding cellar from which came unidentifiable scrabbling and snuffles and, when the wind howled from the north, nearly intelligible mutterings. Up to this point of having some habitable order in the house, I had kept it from entering consciousness. Now, it was crawling out of the black, cob-webbed recesses of the subconscious and waving its extremities in my face.

I have a phobia about spiders, while my wife can actually hold them in her hands. I am humiliated to have to ask her to remove them whenever they climb up into the sink, and endure a pitying, slightly admonishing look, as I shrink away with a resigned shrug.

Predictably, it was my wife who thought it was high time I cleared out the cellar. Those brief moments standing at the top of the stairs had left me with an impression of a hostile realm with a gothic flavour. It was the place where unknown creatures dwelt and subterranean streams seeped and sluggishly flowed; a murky fantasy world visited by children, crying aloud in their sleep. I was all for leaving the untouchable untouched.

I attempted a democratic approach to the problem. I pointed out that I had been responsible for all concreting, plumbing, tiling, wiring and fitting of cupboards, and my wife had taken on the planting, hoeing, raking and planning of the garden, and so it seemed more appropriate for her to head up the cellar clearance.

She wanted to know how this privilege fell under the heading of garden duties. Wasn't it, she pointed out, an inside rather than an outside task?

I pointed out that we had never been inside the cellar, it was not habitable and could only be reached via the garden now that the trap door had been screwed down.

She said 'nonsense', and that won the argument. So we agreed to share the job, and told our seventeen-year-old son he was also a volunteer.

Next came the strategic planning. I suggested that since she was so much better with spiders, she had better deal with the cobwebs that covered the entrance. She reminded me that I was probably better with mice and, in any case, what if there were snakes?

We turned to our son, who declined to even talk about the subject, saying his morbid fear of all beasts would only permit him to work outside. He was happy to arrange a large bonfire to burn everything, but beyond that we could forget it.

I had no alternative but to bite the philosophical bullet, and prepared myself for the worst. It was obvious I would need protection. I dug out all the oldest, bulkiest clothes I could find to make myself impenetrable to tooth, fang and mandible.

At around eleven o'clock on that sweltering sunny day, I waddled towards the creaky old studded door of the *cave* attired in three layers of woollen jumper, a pair of old serge trousers over long-johns, feet crammed into an ancient pair of boots that curled up at the toes in quaintly medieval fashion, and, to complete the ensemble, a battered straw hat and voluminous apron.

My wife bound her hair in a large scarf, tied a handkerchief over her nose like a bank robber and wore thick rubber gloves. Our son chose undersized trousers and shirt, short waterproof boots, from which his limbs projected like those of a circus-attired gibbon, and a cap turned back to front. He seemed inexplicably content with his appearance and hummed the signature tune from The A Team.

We stood, all three, in front of the *cave* door; a modern version of the three musketeers, fully armed with various long-handled garden tools and a well thought-out plan of attack.

It was my task to lead the assault by making as great a

commotion as possible as I thrust open the door, which would frighten the rodents into retreating to the darkest inner recesses. My wife would then rush past me to brush aside all the cobwebs at the entrance and sweep all the spiders off the beams with her broom. She would then stand aside as I came from behind firing my pressure-hosed insecticide gun comprehensively in all directions, and more especially at anything that moved.

Our son was to stand at the door with a rake and hit anything that tried to escape. It was to be a 'rush in, rub out, and rush out again' offensive.

It was executed with the efficiency of an SAS manoeuvre. No arachnid, rodent or serpent could have withstood that onslaught. We were taking no prisoners. Having driven all resistance back, the next stage was to lay waste their rabbit-hutch 'village'. We dragged these out of the gloomy recesses and flung them into the sunlight, where our brave offspring mercilessly threw them onto a heap of kindling ready to become a blazing inferno. At each foray there was a continuous covering burst of insecticide killer.

Finally, only the army of bottles arrayed on the stone shelf was left to attack. The battle was conducted on a scorched earth strategy, and, just in case there were any desperate snipers ready to spring out at us, I handed the insecticide gun over to my wife as I gathered armfuls of the bottles and threw them on the grass outside.

Once the last bottle had been brought out, we beat a hasty retreat and closed the door on the scene of destruction. If the cellar had not been directly under the living room, we would have tossed in a hand-grenade for good measure. During the whole exercise we had seen not a single rodent or serpent; the evil cowards had obviously all gone to ground in the face of such odds.

There lay the spoils of war; five rabbit hutches and two hundred and fifty bottles. I stripped the battle gear off. There was a feeling of exultant victory in the air as we gazed around us at the results.

I strode among the casualties of war and inspected them. The bottles had been used to preserve every conceivable vegetable you could imagine. 'Preserve' was no longer appropriate, for most of the contents were unrecognisable, and certainly inedible. There was something particularly gothic about the pickled walnuts, looking like a collection of shrunken brains. How the original owner had managed to stuff them into those thin-necked lemonade and wine bottles was a mystery.

Our next task was to carry these bottles up to where the refuse collectors could collect them. By now the sun was almost directly overhead, and we were glad that the steps to the top were in the shade. We emerged into the blazing sun to place the bottles in serried ranks in front of the gates.

Having stripped down to shorts and sandals now, we picked up the bottles four or five at a time, and trudged up and down the steps with measured tread and stooped backs, like Pharaoh's slaves. Each time we emerged from the shadows, we joined the mad dogs in the midday sun, which had created an oven of a day.

I always find that difficult tasks are rendered more tolerable by entering into a dramatic flight of fancy. The script emerged:

'In abject pain and misery, we dragged our feet over the hot furnace of the sands, shoulders hunched forward, as the overseer's whip cracked above us and sliced into our shoulders. We groaned in agony as we trudged up the steps for the tenth time. There it was again! The cracking whip.'

Hold on a minute; what whip? Something was cracking, for sure! This was becoming a little too 'virtual'. There it was again. An explosive sound up at the top of the steps! The monotonous adagio of scuffed sandals on the steps came to a sudden halt. We craned our necks and looked up in time to see a wide arc of green liquid bursting forth. Another crack! A sharp, splintering sound, and another explosive fountain of multi-coloured liquid rose up.

I was about to rush up top when a series of explosions broke out. We were under guerrilla attack; Nature was fighting back.

More explosions, this time clearly identified as a diabolical new weapon of rocketed vegetables. I turned on my heels and fled down the steps again.

We stood at a safe distance, watching the liquid firework display, realising now that we were seeing the effect of the sun on the fermented contents of the bottles, rendering them lethal hand-grenades. There they stood, unflinching heroic martyrs awaiting their destiny at they targeted anyone foolish enough to approach, with an indisciminately flung fiendish tomato slurry, a hail of petit-pois and barrage of mange-tout. Shoulder to shoulder, they stood proudly erect in the burning sun, making their brave last stand. Some exploded autonomously, some fell from the blast of their comrades. They would take with them anyone who dared to approach, and perish with honour in the process.

From the cries of alarm from some unaware neighbours, it was obvious that the bottle army had cut off all access to the village, and forced them to beat a hasty retreat. There was only one way to win the day. I clambered round to the other side of the house to gain a new vantage point from the rear of the action, closely followed by wife and son.

After some swift emergency briefing behind the lines, the only solution seemed to be to smother the enemy action by throwing a huge tarpaulin over them. Even if it did not immediately halt the explosions it would severely inhibit their firing range.

And thus it was that the enemy were finally foiled. Racing towards them like a war-stricken refugee weaving my way towards the gate, I flung the blue plastic sheet over the suicidal troops. At last the victory was mine. The corks continued to pop for some time, but the explosions were dampened, and eventually there was silence.

As soon as the sun had gone down beyond the barn roof, we were able to approach the killing fields with impunity to complete the final mopping-up operation. We extracted all remaining corks, emptied the lethal contents onto the compost heap and placed the empty bottles in the shade. At last we could retire from the fray. Our wounds were thankfully only psychological, and could be cured with a couple of pastis.

No doubt, down in the bar that evening they would all be saying, '*Ah, les anglais!*' Ah, well, that was inevitable.

But for us we had exorcised the last vestige of the previous owner's eccentric legacy. It must be said, however, that she had not gone lightly into the dark. The end had come, 'not with a whimper, but a bang!'

12

Festival Time

Everyone we had spoken to, French and British alike, had enthused about the annual folklore festival held in a small town called Confolens, situated at the top right corner of the Charente. This was something you had to drop tools for, no matter what urgent DIY plans you had drawn up.

As the name of the town implies, it stands at the confluence of two rivers, one of them the Vienne, wide, deep and easy flowing, and the other the Goire, a chattering stream bouncing its way down a ravine from the Monts de Blonde in a last sprint under an ancient arched bridge. During the dry summer periods it tends to sneak in with a trickle next to a tiny civic park with pollarded trees where you can adjust your inner clock to the slow meander of the river.

Confolens is a thriving town with a large market hall in a spacious square surrounded by restaurants. On one side one can dine on terraces overlooking the river, and watch canoeists paddle their way upstream. A medieval bridge spans the river between the old and new sectors. Originally the only way across for horse and cart, it is now reserved for pedestrians since the modern bridge was built a little further downstream. Small back streets with an antique shop or two and small tea shops and restaurants wind up the side of the hill from the centre. Pelargoniums trail over windowboxes from houses that nudge each other in communal intimacy. It is picturesque enough as a town with a modestly tourist air about it, and possesses one of the best information centres I have seen.

Sometime during the first two weeks in August the town is completely transformed into a throbbing centre for international folk-singing and dance. Flags and bunting, loudspeakers and booking offices take over, and the main market square is filled with scaffolding supporting banked benches that face a huge stage erected in front of the covered market. This is flanked on both sides by two raised dais for musicians.

At the opening celebration of the festival, a flame is lit in a large receptacle, raised aloft by a pillar to one side of the stage, reminding one of the Olympic Games. The entire assembly of dancing and singing troupes file onto the platform as they are announced on the tannoy system to the accompaniment of stirring music. (One memory that will be eternally etched on my mind is that of a huge inflated globe supported on the backs of two Africans in full national regalia, which was revolved to reveal the part of the world appropriate to the troupe making its entrance. It was a breathtaking piece of theatre that made our planet seem smaller and larger at the same time.)

And every year, at the end of the festival, the flame is extinguished in a moving ceremony in which brotherhood of nations is proclaimed and rather optimistically promised.

In the ten days between, the whole town is dedicated to the festival, during which every civic building of any appropriate size becomes a concert hall. The most joyous occasions are when the whole town, every corner, small square, even T-junction becomes a performance arena around which crowds cluster like medieval spectators at travelling fairs. The resplendent colours of the various nations are astonishing and the gaiety is incomparably infectious. On such open days, which are called *Ville en fête*, the troupes make a grand entry over the new bridge in a mile long cavalcade, each one with a member in the vanguard holding their flag aloft and the country's name clear for all to see.

It was a moving experience to see for the first time, nations coming from behind the Iron Curtain to join the wicked Capitalist Western World. Politics has no place or influence in the festival, and artists from all corners of the world sing and dance together however ideologically opposed they may be.

The range is incredible, from Maori war-dances that include seated canoeists gyrating on their buttocks, overseen by a warrior in loincloth rudely shaking his extended tongue at the audience (the more he wagged the greater the roar of applause), to American tap dances and hoe-downs from Salt Lake City. From Hungarian stately waltzes and passionate gipsy violins to Rwandan circle chants, all related to a vibrant extant culture.

One evening concert we chose to attend in a large gymnasium included performances by groups from Nepal, Spain and Romania. The venue was half a mile up a road climbing up to the outskirts of the town. We found a verge to park our car half way and covered the final stage on foot. As we joined the trudging file of like-minded folk, we were aware of four fire engines passing in some haste and turning off ahead of us. It was only when we arrived at the gymnasium that we realised it was here that the *pompiers* had been making for, with some appearance of urgency, one must say.

The building was completely surrounded by their engines, and the men, fully kitted out in combat attire, were gesticulating towards the windows. We expected to see flames belching forth, and wondered why no one was winding out the hoses, until a bystander informed us it was just a precautionary measure.

Apparently, the firemen were very unhappy about the wide-open pivoting windows, regarding them as a potential lethal hazard.

It was hardly the kind of thing you wanted to hear before you entered a hall to attend a concert, and we did feel that there was an element of overkill to send four fire engines on such an exercise. However, nobody in the waiting crowd seemed too surprised or worried, and we got the impression that this was standard procedure.

The inspection over, and the offending windows closed, doors were free to be thrown open and we were carried unceremoniously through them by the surging throng, like grains of sand through the waist of an hourglass.

Once in, our first impression of any potential lethal hazard was not that of being incinerated but of being suffocated to death. The sun had beaten down on the building all day and it was like a furnace. The seats were laid out as tightly as a newly minted pack of cards.

Naturally, our seats were in the middle of the row already packed with people, and we had to run the gauntlet, employing the aggression of an SAS assault combined with the contortions of Houdini in order to reach them. Everybody's knees were pressed hard into the back of the seat in front, and the only way to make any headway was to get everyone to raise their knees and lean sideways like so many Towers of Pisa. Headway was hardly the word; the head was the only part we did not employ to reach our seats. Elbowing fulsome bosoms and bulging midriffs aside, we straddled the knees of the aged, unable to decide whether full frontal or vulnerable backside was less offensive to the neighbouring members of the audience. Inevitably, we all landed on someone's lap at some stage in the exercise to cries of '*Allez-oop!*' Finally we flopped into our seats, smiled apologetically to our immediate neighbours, just as the show began.

The first part of the evening was taken up with circle dancing, to the accompaniment of a thousand flapping paper fans made out of programmes.

During a display of gymnastic toe-waving by the Nepalese circle, a young boy decided he was in agonising need of a visit to the urinal to unload the cooling lemonade he had earlier consumed. The entire hall focused their attention on his row as everybody bobbed up and down like a poorly rehearsed chorus line to let him pass, an action repeated five minutes later at his return. Embarrassed grins and philosophical grimaces attended his interruption. The circle of dancers continued to gyrate and wave handkerchiefs persistently into each other's faces until, at last, they unwound into one long line and took their last bow to considerable applause.

The enthusiasm of the audience was as much an expression of relief at being allowed out of the oven for the first interval as an appreciation of the artistry. Ice-creams and chilled colas were pounced on, and feelings of panic overcame the end of the queue at the possibility of it all being sold out before they got to the counter.

Everyone fanned their faces, necks and armpits with their programmes as they sucked voraciously on their ice-lollies and cones, until the bell signalled the second visit to the sauna. This time we dived into our seats to avoid inconveniencing or even injuring the elderly, considering the way we had dumped our buttocks on their laps the last time.

I was particularly looking forward to the Spanish dancing which always seemed so full-blooded. I was not disappointed.

They began in stately fashion, the row of men standing like ramrods, backs slightly arched and stomachs held in, with hands on waists, and revolving slowly like vertical roasts on spits, the women swaying back and forth as they peered over their fans with passionate provocation. This slow movement seemed eminently sensible considering the stifling, clammy air. They were used to such heat in Spain, but would have opened the windows, I told myself.

Hardly had the thought occurred before there was a sudden violent outburst of heel tapping, and a man who, until that moment, had been as immobile as a wax image on the side of the stage, let out a piercing cry of pain to guitar accompaniment. From then on it was the most aggressive passionate exchange between the sexes that I have ever witnessed. Each side was bent on challenging the other with their excessive proclamations. The men looked disdainfully down their noses at the women, who turned their backs scornfully and flounced their skirts at the men. The flamenco singer, who sounded as if his foot had been trodden on by an elephant, was obviously lamenting that all this heel stamping would bring them to a bad end, and there would be tears before bedtime.

The choreography could be translated thus:

The men (standing side on to the women, turning their heads towards them, and stamping) – 'I snort down my nose at your pathetic attempt to manifest your passion. So there!'

The women (tossing their heads back, and stamping their heels staccato) – 'And I grind your lukewarm amorous attempts into the dust by stabbing the floor very fast with my heels.'

The men (looking the women up and down dismissively) – 'I defy you to show a fraction of the love I feel. There, see! Even my constant stamping cannot extinguish the embers of my passion!'

The women (revolving on the spot) – 'I gyrate my torso and thrust my buttocks at you to show my utter contempt for your tepid love. Stop looking at my knees when I pull my skirt up to my thighs!'

The men (determinedly staring) – 'I will look at your knees if I want to, and especially if it inflames your anger. Your contempt is a total turn on!'

The women (drawing themselves up to full height and advancing nose to nose with the men) – 'And your snorting excites me to distraction!'

I conjecture that any such energetic prelude to love-making would render the participants incapable of its performance.

The flamenco singer on the side of the stage could hardly contain himself by this time, for he launched into a graphic description of the dreadful consequences of such passion. The dance rose in a crescendo of murderous intention and then suddenly came to an end. Teeth were flashed at the audience and we applauded madly. I was certain, however, that such characters, once uninhibited by the presence of an audience, would inflict terrible harm on each other the moment they got in the wings.

Another interval, and another opportunity to wring our handkerchiefs out, apply ice-cream to various parts of the body and breathe in enough air to tide us over in the final section of the evening. This was taken up by the Romanians, the most morosely frenetic troupe I had, and still have, ever seen. They were incredibly keen, and began playing before half the audience were back in their seats. In fact they appeared to be oblivious to them, so deeply involved were they in their soulful rendering. The violinist cradled his instrument across his forearm and rocked back and forth on his heels with furrowed brow and intense expression, as if suffering from a painful condition. The trumpeter kept his eyes shut whenever he played, and when he was not, stared unblinking over the heads of the audience like a blind man. The kaval player blew down his minute pipe like a boy blowing through a pea-shooter. (Occasionally he would change over to the pan pipes, and pass his lips over them with such velocity one felt they were in danger of being worn away.) But by far the most energetic was the cymbalon player, striking the keyboard with his tiny felted hammers like a demented panel-beater.

The music was so shapeless and drawn out, it was difficult for most (and for me impossible) to detect a melody. Occasionally there was a rallentando section, which allowed the musicians to catch up with each other. Having re-synchronised, there would follow a tremolo passage like a swarm of bees deciding in which direction to fly off, leading into the final passage played at breakneck speed.

The end came so abruptly we were all taken off guard. After a pause, we clapped tumultuously, most conscious of the fact that they had managed, miraculously, to finish in concert and in one piece. They took their bow and exited as swiftly as they had played.

As we emerged into the now fading evening light, we were amazed to be waylaid by these very same musicians, who thrust recordings of their music into our hands with repeated demands, in gutteral tones, to buy. Their faces expressed a fierce need, and self-defence compelled us to hand over our francs. In prohibition Chicago, these dark-skinned, side-burned characters would have made offers of concrete overcoats you could not refuse.

Later, we learned that they had only been allowed out of Romania on the understanding that they brought back foreign currency to the Ceausescu regime. They must have been under some considerable pressure to comply. Had we known, we might have been encouraged to buy more.

We left Confolens aware of having been seated in sweaty discomfort in a dangerously overcrowded hall, while time flew by. The Nepalese had brought a breath of snow-capped mountains, herded goats and rural simplicity; the Spanish had depicted a world of disdainful elegance and noble, aggressive passions; and the Romanians had taken us to crowded smoke-filled restaurants, where fierce waiters in rolled-up sleeves rushed round serving goulash and vodka.

They had all contributed to a feeling of human oneness and to a comprehension that song and dance can transcend with a powerful immediacy all the differences that the various national literatures point to.

I am well aware of having fallen short here of capturing its true power to move. Long may the world continue to play music together in Confolens, while the politicians play dangerous games with each other.

13

Skeletons in the Cupboard

Once our neighbour, Jeannine, had grown accustomed to her imprudent British neighbours, she took a lively interest in what we were doing to our little bit of French heritage.

Being the first British she had encountered, we were a new window on the world for her. But once familiar with our funny ways, she became a good friend who kept an eye on things when we were away, watered plants in dry spells, and kept us informed of what was going on in the village. In common with all country folk she was into gossip, and would share it with us, as with anyone, whether we were familiar with the subject or not.

She was a creature of habit, and the shape of her day varied little. Apart from domestic chores, it involved a walk down the steps to the *superette*, and *boulangerie*, tidying the entrance to the cemetery, tending to her husband's grave and watering the flowers there; all punctuated by brief exchanges of news with passing neighbours, the postman or the refuse collectors.

Once a week she allowed the peripatetic priest, who gave confession and communion in four parishes, to use her house to teach the local children their catechism. It also provided a welcome break for her to chat with the Father, and to offer him a glass of home-made walnut wine to help him cope with his boisterous young charges. It may well have disposed him to perform his duties well, but from having tasted the potion myself, I am not sure it would have greatly assisted his efficiency in them.

Jeannine's three children had flown to other parts of France to succeed in the world, and they would visit her from time to time, especially in the summer. She loved to see her grandchildren, who were all growing up in a world she neither understood nor embraced, believing that it offered them unimaginable things that were not proper to seek.

'The young can't wait to have anything; they must have everything now. In our day, what you couldn't afford you did without. But today, they don't believe in God, and want other things instead.'

Although it was quite difficult to grasp her not very rational thinking, I understood her to be saying that religion went out with the tougher life of her times. I once suggested that maybe today's youth are not quite as bad as they are painted. She uttered a deep-throated humourless laugh, adopted a gargoyle expression, and looked at me as if I were mad. I backed down with an apologetic shrug, ready to concede that modern youth is encouraged to be pretty selfish, and that the world offers them more seductive temptations than ever before.

Her opinions were constructed on her own life experience, and were not to be contested, although what God had to do with it all I was not as sure as she. I would never say it to her, but it seemed to be more to do with the traditional church.

I have little difficulty in accepting the possibility that the world is not improving morally, but I look down at the classically beautiful Romanesque church, an ancient relic of the Age of Belief, and wonder what on earth it can say to the youth of today, bombarded as they are by adverts for the 'good life' down 'easy street'. How can it begin to sell Saint Augustine's work ethic to the unemployed young French? In any case, there must be something more exciting to say about God outside the mouldy stones of this eleventh-century abbatial monument. Certainly, it is an important reminder of a world dedicated to piety and faith that is at low tide in the modern world, but I very much doubt if God can survive in this cold damp church; the mould-covered stones are enough to give you spiritual pneumonia.

Once, when Jeannine's daughter came in the summer with her family from Paris, she complained bitterly of the lack of life in the village she escaped from.

'There are too many old people,' she said, as if this could in any way be avoided in a world that insists on keeping them alive with one of the best health services in the world. 'The young have all left. Even the few who remain would like to go. There is nothing for them but to take over the farms from their parents.' She says this with some aggression, as if we should have recognised this and thought twice before buying a property in the region. She thinks it strange that the English should want to come to this unexciting rural region given over to farming, a place from which she has escaped to make a life for herself.

'This is a sad place to come to, isn't it?' she asks, searching my face suspiciously, as if seeking an ulterior motive. I try to explain that perhaps we are seeking the peace that comes with the predictability from which she escaped. I suggest that the grass is always greener in someone else's pasture. Her eyes glaze in incomprehension.

She is now a Parisienne, with a successful businessman husband, and living in a smart apartment in the city with a vibrant cultural life. However, she has made me review my motives for coming here. If I am seeking peace, am I escaping from something? As a teacher I would have been glad to escape having to be available to cover the duties of civil servant, social worker and instructor all rolled into one; as an actor I would have lost little from the long periods spent waiting for someone to take advantage of my availability; but as a writer I can escape to a haven for positive reasons, not merely propelled by a mid-life crisis.

I would not advise anyone used to an urban life to take up home in the Charente. In fact I have seen some unfortunate results of couples coming out thinking that peace, the good life and ownership of acres of available land will bring happiness. It is one thing to have a secondary residence for short holiday periods –

103

quite another to spend your life out there. Summers are warm and sunny much of the time, but winters can be very cold and damp, and, however well appointed your property, you may feel very cut off.

The Charente suits me so because I am a country lad at heart, and feel I am returning to my roots, or at least to my idea of them. I suspect some affinity of mine with the rural world of both my grandfathers. One, a young boy at the turn of the last century, fled from Broadway in Worcestershire to escape the soul-killing physical drudgery of farm work. The other, a journeyman joiner, avoided rampant unemployment in Montgomeryshire, escaping over the borders into Cheshire.

Leaving aside the inevitable internal combustion engine, there is something about the Charente that suggests late Victorian British landscape, comparable with a blend of Cotswold limestone walls, and the rolling hills and valleys of mid Wales. It is warmer than either of these, however, and the curved russet and clay-coloured Roman tiled roofs found south of Poitiers tell you that this is not Britain.

There are many more scenically dramatic regions in France than this one, much of which rolls up and down in tree-covered folds until it finally spills its last remnants of the Massif Central onto the flat plains that run the length of the Atlantic coast.

I feel at home in the half-familiar countryside that shows me something I carry inside me. But how on earth would I be able to say any of this to Jeannine's daughter? How can I romanticise to her about what she took for granted and finally rejected? What could I tell her of my delight at the warm smell of baked earth as the summer shadows lengthen? Or the 'cris-cris' of the crickets, incessantly ticking away their reminders of time's passage? Or the lowing cattle and bleating sheep in the distance, declaring their acceptance of Nature's lot? And, at night, the barn owl following the same path over our roof from the church tower to the coppice on the banks of the valley. And finally, the clear, gem-studded sky slowly revolving above us to the pulse-beat of a sleeping dormouse. This is just not communicable to her. If it were, she would not have left.

One day Jeannine came over to our gate and, seeing us in the garden, entered and said with a knowing look and a crooked smile, 'You have dug the garden very carefully, yes?'

'We will do, in time, when we can get round to it.'

'You might strike it rich.' She nodded wisely as she caught our close attention. She smiled, enjoying for the moment our incomprehension.

'Elise, my old neighbour, knew how to save her money. It grew into quite a tidy sum over the years.' She passed one hand repeatedly over the other, miming the gathering of coins, and laughed as she continued, 'Yes, you would do well to turn the soil over carefully. You may find something *très intéressante.*'

'What kind of interesting?' I asked. She shrugged and looked wise.

'Her sons did not find anything in the house, so where is it? They went through all the furniture. There was nothing.'

I remembered the furniture and imagined the task they must have given themselves.

'Maybe,' she went on, 'you will be luckier in the garden. She might have buried a fortune over the years. She was always careful with her money; always complaining she was a pauper. She didn't spend a centime.'

'How did she manage, then?'

Jeannine shook her head and reflected. 'It was an illness with her. She was a good enough neighbour,' she added hastily, 'always ready to listen to your worries, but, well – she had this problem.'

'Oh?'

'Elise had ...' and her voice dropped to a whisper in case the birds heard her, 'sticky fingers.' She gave an emphatic nod, and it took a few seconds for the significance to sink in.

As if she had somehow betrayed her former neighbour, she swiftly added, 'She couldn't help herself. It was a compulsion.'

She reflected on this wistfully for a second before chuckling, 'Monsieur and Madame Boudin, who own the *superette*, used to hide behind the shelves whenever Elise went into the shop. They would watch her fill her basket through peepholes between the groceries, and then rush out at the last moment to prevent her leaving without paying. When they managed to reach the door first, she would pretend to search for her purse and say she had forgotten it.'

'How annoying for the shopkeepers and sad for her,' I said.

'It didn't stop there. When she didn't get what she wanted in the shop, she would wait till it closed and then visit everyone to beg for a cup of sugar, flour or a couple of spoons of tea, saying she had forgotten to buy them. In the end, it got so bad that whenever you called on your neighbour, you had to whisper your name through the keyhole, or nobody would answer the door.'

'Good heavens! So the whole village was under siege then?'

'It was like that till she left. She spent nothing and hoarded everything.' Jeannine gave a wicked chuckle as she delivered her final *coup de grâce*.

'She even hoarded René, her husband, when he died.'

I narrowed my eyes and gave her a sideways look.

'No, it is true! She got up to make René his bowl of coffee, and when she shook him and got no response, she realised he had died during the night. She propped him up on the pillows and kept quiet. It was four days later before his drinking *copains* in the bar decided it was time to find out why he hadn't shown his face. They climbed up the path, knocked on the door, and got suspicious when she tried to prevent them entering. When they did get past her there he was, propped up stiff as a board and smelling not too sweet. Even then she protested she had a right to keep him.'

I tried to show some lively appreciation of the jolly little story, while imagining just exactly where he might have been propped up. It turned out, finally, to be where we had placed the kitchen sink, which was some kind of relief.

'It is funny the way some people live, *n'est-ce pas?*' she said with a sigh. I nodded.

'Ah, well, I must be off to do my bit of shopping,' she said. 'But don't forget to dig carefully.'

She ambled down the steps, and as she turned the corner I am not sure, but I think I heard her laugh softly to herself.

14

At a Farmer's Table

November had come round again, wearing a multi coloured head-dress and smoking a pipe of peace. I wore a tee-shirt to work in the garden most of the time, but the evenings were drawing in and winter was around the next bend, making both ends of the day cooler. The dew lay on the lawn till eleven o'clock and by mid-afternoon the mists began to rise off the river below. Vertical spirals of smoke drifted from the village chimneys, the trees lining the banks took on an unkempt look, like tattered hat feathers that had attended too many functions, and distant figures in the fields began to take noticeably bulkier shape as they wrapped themselves round with thicker garments.

The earth gave off a rich odour of damp and decay. A brave cricket practised a bar or two of his summer ballad and, after the desultory burst on his strings, put down his bow and hobbled back to his crevice in the wall, leaving the midges to continue their aerial dance under the plum trees, and the industrious spiders to build their huge trawling nets across the branches. Opalescent over-ripe grapes hung in sensuous plenty on the meandering vines, and there was peace of a kind to savour.

As soon as the sun descended, the air chilled and we hastened inside to light the log fire. The wood-pile was almost depleted, and a visit to my friend Paolo was imperative for our well-being.

We first came into contact with Paolo and Francesca at the infamous wedding breakfast, Paolo being one of those betrayed into surrendering his socks under the axe. During our first Christmas at the house they invited us to a squid stew, a meal that challenged our traditional view of seasonal festive fare. After that, we met several times to discuss what New Year resolutions we had broken and to put the world to rights over an aperitif of Pinneau des Charentes or pastis.

We can look back on a period of mutual aid and trust in which I lent him my cement mixer to build his front wall, and he planted trees in our garden to create shade. He was also my log provider at a reasonable price.

He and Francesca met in Belgium just after the Second World War. Both Italian, and raised in the region near the Yugoslavian border, they made the decision to settle in the Charente and raise cattle and sheep, because of the temperate climate and an extended growing season. It was a good decision, for he lived through a prosperous period during the sixties and seventies, when farmers received generous subsidies.

His house bears witness to this, being a four-bedroom residence of some distinction with a balustrade and curving stairway to the front door that is more typical of modern houses you might find on the banks of the lakes of northern Italy. I do not believe he would get planning permission to build in this style now, since the central authority governing architecture in Paris became purist about regional character in the eighties and nineties. This was probably occasioned largely by the weird ideas foreigners, including the British, had about renovating houses. I am firmly on the side of the French in this, for they probably prevented architectural mayhem.

Two things mark Paolo and Francesca out from their neighbours – Italian Catholicism and heavy accents. Francesca hits her consonants, and especially her 'r's very energetically which makes her sound emphatic about everything. She has a fulsome figure and wears a bun at the back of her head, and her round florid face is characteristic of the traditional Italian *mama*. Paolo complements her with a voice reminiscent of Marlon

110

Brando's Corleone in The Godfather. He is aware of the timbre of his voice, and remarks himself on its rasping quality, blaming it on too much shouting over fields and several throat infections in consecutive frosty winters.

First impressions might mislead you into seeing him as a man of harsh temperament, but quite the opposite is the truth. In fact, everyone in the village refers to him as a clown, and they intend this description as a compliment. He has an openness and a talent to make you smile that would make him a fit candidate for a Fellini film. Or, on account of his constant childish pranks, he might have made a wonderful presenter of children's television programmes. One minute he will transform himself into some weird fiction of his imagination to peer round a door and then pretend to be dragged suddenly from sight by the hand he stretches over his own head; the next moment he may pretend to unscrew his arm at the elbow, in the fashion of early Commedia dell'Arte, to the accompaniment of grotesque facial expressions.

He indulges himself in this creative silliness, and you find it bizarre and endearing at the same time. At such times it is difficult to believe he can ever be serious, but he uses this playfulness to good effect. He was proud to inform me one day, as we sat in his kitchen, that since he took part in the farmers' annual village feasts, there have never been any violent drunken outbursts. He puts that down entirely to his ability to spread good-will around him.

'Nobody thinks of fighting if I am around. They enjoy themselves too much, and stop taking themselves too seriously.'

Overhearing this, Francesca wears a sceptical expression, which advises you to take it all 'with a pinch of salt'. I recognise this as being the typical reaction of most wives when they hear their spouses giving themselves excessive credit.

When Paolo is in more serious mood, his chiselled features, light brown wavy hair, and deep-set eyes between furrowed brow and bony cheeks, all suggest dramatic possibility. In a certain light, he could be a fair-haired version of Jack Palance's gun-slinger in *Shane*; in another, he more reminds you of the comic mime artist Jacques Tati.

He congratulates me on choosing to come to the Charente, but does not fully understand my motives, apart from the benefits of the climate. I don't tell him that I do not understand what I was doing at the time, either. He thinks that most British look for tourist attractions where they can spend their summers. I am able to convince him that I seek no such thing, and he praises me for it. However, he holds some suspicions as to my intentions with regard to the house. Above all, he urges me to preserve its character and age, and the most important features. The one he holds in most reverence is our basement, the *cave*.

'What a magnificent place to keep your wine. It will mature and mellow like a beautiful woman does with age,' he says, as Francesca throws a cool and cynical sideways glance at him.

'It has an even, cool temperature, and there is minimum movement of the damp air. Perfect!'

She grunts and shakes her head in disbelief.

He pronounces his delight at our subterranean miracle in the same hushed tones the pilgrim reserves for the hallowed church precincts containing a saint's bones.

For the umpteenth time, he asks what I propose to do with the *cave*. I reply for the umpteenth time that I propose to put two windows in the north-facing wall overlooking the village, treat all the damp where possible, and seal what cannot be treated behind a false wall at the back. Finally, I tell him, as his eyes open ever wider, that I will channel the stream that oozes out of the walls through under-floor drainage pipes. Then I say, with some defiant finality, it will be a perfect place to sit on summer evenings and listen to the music of Vivaldi.

There is always a pregnant silence, and then he raises his hands and shakes his head in melodramatic despair at the contemplation of such desecration.

'How can you do such a thing?'

112

I refuse to be influenced by his dramatics, and reply in a calm tone.

'I haven't decided yet. But there must be a way to cover the stream. Then we can make it habitable.'

His face crumples as I speak, and he winces and emits a prolonged moan. He looks over at Francesca to appeal to her and is met with a passive shrug. He lines his brow with furrows.

'But then ...' He struggles to cope with his horrific vision, 'the damp will not be able to rise.'

I nod.

'Hmm, hmm. That is precisely the intention.'

'But ...' He swallows hard, 'at least the walls will be left damp, yes?'

'Absolutely not,' I assert, keeping my fixed smile going. 'In fact I may have to insert silicone in parts of the wall to make them non-porous and so keep back the damp that way.'

His face becomes Oedipus about to put out his eyes.

'But, if you do this thing, the walls will not sweat!'

I outface his devastation. 'Absolutely right.'

'Then, I must tell you that what you will do, is tragic.'

He places his head in his hands, but I think I can see him peeping at me through them. I nod wisely for his benefit, and attempt to look contrite, and express my sorrow that posterity will suffer such great loss merely for the sake of our own comfort and protection from rheumatism.

I also refrain from mentioning his own well-appointed residence with central heating, hot and cold water in all bedrooms and a particularly nice dry warm basement. I do not remind him that he wants me to live in conditions he would not, for one second, contemplate for himself.

I reflect for a moment how he might sell my house if he were an estate agent:

An ancient house with superb reminders of the minimal facilities of medieval life. Somewhere to wash, sleep and cook, and lots of sloping garden, giving views of intending marauders. This property is remarkable for its magnificent cold, streaming cellar offering incomparable conditions for wine storage. The porosity of the wall allows full seepage to take place in seasonal downpours. The connoisseur can be confident of maximum condensation and cobwebs. Here is an unrivalled opportunity to own a *cave* of mystic mustiness and delightful damp. Prospective buyers will be required to sign a preservation order.

It is fair to say that it was mainly the Brits who were able to appreciate the opportunities in the primitive nature of such property. This was because the French had lived in primitive conditions for decades, and had had enough of it all. They hold no fond memories of zinc baths, oil stoves, earth floors and endemic arthritis. They want the full modern life up and running, and they want it yesterday. It is on this account that so much of their heritage has fallen into foreign hands. However, they do seem to have watched the Brits apply their DIY skills over a period, and are now beginning to see new possibilities themselves. A few have even made a business of renovating property as an investment to amplify their pensions.

Paolo has only been a farmer. It is too late for him to think on these lines, and he complains about the paucity of his prospective pension. Under current French law, the moment he retires he will be forbidden to raise animals, except for a few sheep for his own consumption. Consequently, he has developed a side-line of scrap metal and bric-a-brac, which he stores in a huge corrugated-roofed hangar. It is an unkempt Aladdin's Cave of rusty farm implements that someone, somewhere, might recognise as useful some time or other.

He views his old age in a rather dismal light, but I am aware that his pessimism is rather overplayed. I notice his brand new petrol-driven, sit-on lawn mower and ask him, *en passant* if he is pleased with his new possession. He looks at me with some suspicion and straightaway adopts a woeful expression, saying it is a great pity his age forces him to spend his small savings to invest in such a thing.

'The doctor advised me to get it,' he says. 'It is the only way I can keep my land cut back. I cannot afford to pay anyone to do it.' He adopts a suitably crestfallen expression and nods gloomily. 'Ah, age is a problem.' He says the same thing to all his neighbours in case they think he has money to burn. He reinforces this impression of poverty by launching into all his financial grievances, including the lowering of subsidies to a level that, according to him, hardly covers the cost of animal feed or fertilisers. He also goes on at some length about the crippling income tax.

'No wonder there are strikes and blockades on the roads. Is it surprising the farmers are making themselves a public nuisance?'

I nod sympathetically, remembering having been stopped at the ports twice and, additionally, a few times on the open road leading south. I also remember the attack on English consignments of lamb, and put it to him that this might not be seen as supportive of *entente cordiale*. He characteristically raises his hands in horror and declares his hope that no one could possibly believe him capable of such behaviour. But, he adds, 'It is not against the English *confrères* that they do such things; they are only attacking the policies of the French Government.'

I reflect that it is a bizarre thing that when the French farmers want to attack their government, they do it by turfing English produce onto the road. This is another subject that is best left alone for the sake of tact and diplomacy. Paolo has no such qualms, and launches into English politics and culture.

'Now that *La Dame de Fer* Madame Thatcher, has gone, *Grande Bretagne* can enter Europe, *oui*?'

I tell him I do not know what difference it will have made, but remind him Britain has not been invaded since 1066, and has become rather insular since then. He grips my arm and nods, grinning.

'Ah!' he smirks, 'The royal family. What will happen now that they do not have competition from Madame Thatcher?'

I have not the least idea, but apparently he does, and is ready and eager to inform me.

'It is the Conservatives who keep the royal family in business. But now that Princess Diana has gone, they will not survive. Tony Blair will get rid of the nobility and then fox-hunting will disappear.'

With as much nonchalance as I can muster, bearing in mind that I am not sure of the relevance or causal connection in his thinking I ask, 'Isn't there a class system in France, then?'

'*Mais oui*,' he concedes, and then adds, 'but it is based on education and income; not on birthright or tradition.'

'Haven't I seen press photos of fox hunting in France?' I ask.

'*Mais oui*, but that is around Paris, and Paris isn't France. You can even find imbeciles that support the French royal family round there. But, thank the Lord, ever since the revolution the real French learned to rule their hearts with their heads. The English government will always protect Queen Elizabeth's family because it provides lots of fun, and distracts everyone from the political mistakes. The French prefer to blame their government without such distraction.'

He pokes the table with his fingers to preface the next stage of his argument.

'I tell you what happened in Italy. Mussolini was a sincere man – a bit of a criminal, I agree, but very sincere. He had good ideas for the Italian people but he wanted to make his family into a royal household. In the end, it was this they did not forgive him. He took them into a war they did not want, but if he had not been so ambitious, they would have forgiven him. No one blames the English royal family for anything like that. They just wonder how they can make so many mistakes about their marriage partners.'

He nods at me and raises his eyebrows to show his earnest sincere opinion.

'In my opinion, it is time to become a republic like us.'

'And then what?' I ask.

'Who knows? At least you'd be able to start again, and come into Europe without looking back. Maybe it will happen sooner than you think, and then you won't have to chop their heads off. But, in any case, they are doing a good job of sacking themselves without help from anyone else.'

As we round off the evening by finishing a bottle of his indifferent Pineau des Charentes, I ask him what his politics are. He starts by reminding me he is a peasant. In this he has nothing in common with Van Gogh's potato-eaters or Millet's gleaners with their slack jaws and bent backs. But he is reminding me he is a proud and astute owner of land, who has always put his trust in the returns of the soil. His income has always come from what he has husbanded, and he distrusts anything else, especially politics.

He sums it up: 'Politicians may make mistakes or cheat, but the land always stays the same and is faithful. No one can prophesy what the seasons will bring, but at least all the farmers are in the same boat, and are responsible for the yield they gather. The trouble begins as soon as politicians, who know nothing about farming, tell us how to tend the land.'

Whenever I visit Paolo I am convinced that if I were a journalist, I could employ most of what he says as leaders for tomorrow's newspaper editorials. He is an amateur philosopher who gathers his reflections on life from a collection of encyclopaedias kept on shelves next to his hearth, and searches for questions that he can answer in his own way. He is a jester, who loves to play childish games because he believes in their edifying effect. He is earnest and complex and moody, and I have never seen him without soil under his fingernails.

As we say goodnight, he tells me that he will deliver two metres of wood tomorrow, and charge me three hundred francs. Friendship is one thing, and business is another.

Good as his word, the following morning I find he has dumped the logs at my gate, and next to them, a large bag of chestnuts to roast on my fire.

15

Raising the Roof

It is as inadvisable for a tortoise to try to survive without a shell, as it is to modernise the interior of your home without a proper roof over your head. It will all end badly.

During our internal renovation we became increasingly conscious of a lot of unused space under the roof, and began to feel cheated that when the architect drew up the plans, he had designated it *non habitable*. We had decided not to use it to store animal fodder for the winter, for which it was originally intended. However, we knew that certain wee beasties had ignored the architect, and had taken up permanent squatting rights there.

I peered over the rim of the trap door occasionally and the vision that repeatedly impinged on my mind was, let us say, disquieting. The whole roof was bowed in the middle and the centre of the apex was supported by an assortment of offcuts and branches placed at unlikely angles, some still carrying their bark. Now that we were completely ensconced in the house, the roof increasingly pressed down on our consciousness.

We learned, through a neighbouring English carpenter friend, about another builder who had recently escaped across the Channel to settle in the next town. I found his name in the telephone directory and rang him. The voice at the other end had something of a West Country accent. It said its name was Martin, confessed to being able to deal with roofs, and said it would come round to discuss requirements the following day.

The voice arrived in time for coffee, and turned into a slim, long-haired fellow with the staring eyes and fulsome beard of an Old Testament prophet. He wore a permanent smile on his face, and assured us, at every stage of our negotiations, of the complete impossibility of any problem arising. He would complete the job with ease, and could start immediately.

Taken off-guard by his eagerness, I asked how much the renewal of the roof would cost. He smiled even more broadly, and said, 'That'll need a bit o' costin'. 'Ave to get back to you on this one.'

'We only want a rough estimate,' I urged. 'More of a feasibility exercise. Can you give us that now?'

'No problem. Just a case o' workin' out the man hours and the workforce I'd need to hire.'

'We just want a rough idea to work around. No need for detailed costing.'

The smile never faltered as he avoided giving the slightest hint of money.

'Leave it to me. I'll sort it out, don't you worry.'

I guess if you had asked him for the date set for your execution, he would, with the broadest smile, have told you not to worry. He left promising that, whatever the cost, he would give us the best price, which I thought a trifle ambiguous.

When the *devis* arrived a couple of days later, it was the highest best price imaginable. I had no idea of the likely cost, never having been involved in such a large project, or worked out wages for hired labour. However, my wife said she thought he had an honest smile. I wondered how you could come to such a conclusion if you had never seen any other expression on his face. I said I liked to see a man in contrasting moods before making a judgement about his character, and confessed to having a problem with anyone who appeared that happy all the time. She countered this by wondering how I could question a man's right to smile; it might well show he was at peace with himself. I put it to her that it would be difficult not to smile when you had the prospect of receiving a cheque the size he was asking, and added that I would not find it hard to be at peace with myself in the same situation. As always, she brought the debate to an end with the inescapable question. What alternative had we, if we wanted to prevent the roof from collapsing on us? In addition, was there not the real possibility of creating extra essential living space? At such moments I recognise my Waterloo. But there is always need of a short period of frowning silence for reflection, while I balance the cost, review the alternatives, bite the bullet, and capitulate.

I rang Martin, accepted his price and, *en passant*, informed him of my willingness to join the workforce, hoping it might occur to him to lower the cost. He told me – no doubt with his peaceful smile – that he had already counted on that.

Three days later, at an unsociable hour, a Renault van pulled up outside the gates and four men in blue dungarees, windcheaters and woolly hats got out. Led by Martin, they loped towards me, looking ready to engage in a bank robbery. The first one to fetch a nylon stocking out of his pocket would have seen me off.

Greeting them with a cheery *'Bonjour!'* and a jaunty *'Bienvenu à tous!'* I awaited the returned chorus of *'bonjours!'*

Instead I received variously, 'Hi!', 'How do!', 'There you go, then!' and 'Is the kettle on?'

They were all Brits, who had been gathered from behind the stones of various surrounding villages by the scent of spare cash to be made. I was impressed that so many in the building trade could be called upon at such short notice. How encouraging it was to find so many good men and true, ready to ply their honourable trade to renew a compatriot's roof in the Charente.

It took only minutes to learn that the workforce consisted of an ex-member of the Civil Defence, an ex-publican and an ex-wine retailer, all of whom had left their own DIY exploits to earn money for their next outlay on materials. So, in effect, I was employing a group of do-it-yourselfers to do what I could not do myself, so that they could continue their do-it-yourself themselves. I just hoped Martin's professional supervision would be sufficient.

The first stage required brute force rather than skill. This was to strip the roof tiles off, and throw them in the back of Martin's van to be dumped as hardcore for a new surface he was laying at the entrance of his drive. Two grades of workmanship were required for this; unskilled and naively intrepid. The first category stood on the roof, throwing tiles with wild abandon shouting, 'Watch your backs!' while the second category, constantly hunkering down under fire, wheel-barrowed the shovelled tiles up the plank-covered steps, shouting 'Mind where you're chucking it!' Needless to say, I found myself in the second category.

At the commencement of the roof stripping, my wife was instructed to make a commitment to stay indoors or out, but on no account to pass from one to the other without observing strict regulations. Martin was obviously a man of courage, for he lined my wife up with the rest of the troops and ordered her to follow proper procedure at all times during the tile bombardment. Failure to do so might incur heavy casualties. He delivered his instructions like a general on the eve of battle.

'It is absolutely imperative that if you 'ave to make a sortie,' (pause for this to sink in) 'you make your intentions clear, and never,' (heavily emphasised) 'make a single move until we give the all-clear. Always,' (raking the faces of everyone present) 'give clear indications and,' (raising an admonishing finger) 'wait until the tiles die down before making your next move. Failure to comply may incur heavy casualties.'

We all nodded our passionate agreement, were dismissed to our posts and the battle commenced. From then on, tiles flew incessantly and the shattered shrapnel was perpetually scooped into barrows, as we ducked and dived and trundled up the steep steps.

Mid-morning, my wife put Martin's regulations to the test by thrusting a broom through the window and shouting for 'permission to exit'. Straightway the shouts went down the line with military precision: 'Lady coming through the door!' This triggered instant statuesque silence.

'Permission to pass granted!' And the lady, wearing her gardening gloves, picked her way gingerly over the debris to gather her spray of mint and thyme from the vegetable plot. Once safely out of the firing line, the bombardment continued until, minutes later, as she hove into sight through the wisteria, the regulation cry went out again, 'Lady going back through door!' and 'Permission to pass!' as she re-entered with her bouquet of herbs.

During these interludes the silence was as deafening as the clatter of cascading tiles, and you could sense Martin straining at the leash, through his flashing teeth, to rescue the lost seconds. Even when the cry went out, 'Lady coming through door! Permission to bring out tray of tea and biscuits!' Martin found it necessary to remind the troops of the regulation time allotted for breaks.

We were working to a deadline from the word go. Pallets of new tiles and huge beams were expected by the end of the day, and space had to be made for them in the courtyard. For the tile-flingers it was a backbreaking job, and for the wheel-barrowers it was the shoulders and calves that tightened into knots under the strain of pushing their loads uphill. By the end of the day, I discovered throbbing muscles I never knew I had.

Once the tiles had been removed, the second stage involved stripping the horizontal battens off the rafters. The tile-flingers became javelin-throwers, as we menials below gathered the battens and carried them away to make a bonfire at the far end of the garden.

When the new replacement tiles and timber did arrive at the end of the day, the exhausted workforce left them precisely where the driver had dropped them off, and drifted into the twilight like the usual suspects called to an identity parade.

The second day had a dramatic feel about it. I was awed by the thought of the huge main cross-beam that bridged the upper storey being sliced through. It must have been there for centuries, and removing it felt as if we were smudging out a piece of history. Martin came with only two other hands this time, the ex-member of Civil Defence having been given leave of absence for missions of his own. We were not short-handed, however, for we were into the technological stage now. Martin carried an immense chainsaw, and without the least sense of occasion proceeded to cut into all the rafters and purlins, leaving us to gather up the debris and throw it into the courtyard. The exposed wooden skeleton was being cut up to make a void where once there was a roof, and I do not think I ever resented Martin's smile more than I did during this time.

Finally, there remained only the huge cross-beam resting on the north and south walls effectively dividing in two any living area we had in mind. A square twenty-foot oak beam, eighteen inches thick, is heavier than anyone imagines, and over the ages becomes as hard as iron. There was no way it could be removed in one piece, being far too heavy for even four of us to lift. The only solution was to cut it into three pieces, which we could then hoist over the edge into the courtyard on one side, and into the lower garden on the other side. The danger was that the pieces, as they were cut, might crash down on to the floor and bring the ceiling below down with them. My wife, when she heard of this possibility, opted to sit in the caravan, refusing to play host to a large piece of oak that might drop in.

The only way to prevent such a catastrophe was to jam blocks under the middle of the beam, and have all hands supporting the end of the shorter piece as the saw cut into it. This would prevent the wood binding on the blade as it dropped under its own weight. We grunted and groaned, taking the weight until Martin gave his warning shout as the blade completed its cut. A third of the beam's length was then slowly and laboriously lowered. A wooden plate was laid on the wall where it had rested, and over this we eased the huge weight little by little, until it dropped down with a mighty thud into the courtyard below. Without the plate as a weight distributor, the beam would certainly have made a large section topple over the wall with it. You could feel the tremor as the beam hit the courtyard, testimony to its destructive power.

In this fashion the three sections of beam were removed and dropped to the ground, to lie like giant warriors fallen in battle. From this point reconstruction became a safer process, especially for those working below. The major task was to get the new twenty-foot pine beams up and over the walls in the opposite direction. But Martin had made this possible within the bounds of our combined strength by constructing the apex support beam of two lengths, which he would bolt together when *in situ*. This would enable the apex to carry the whole weight of the roof and give us full standing height over most of the floor area. It was now safe to move around without fear of an aerial attack. The laying of the beams and rafters was skilled labour, and I was no longer expected to be part of the workforce.

It was at this point that my wife took on her new role of film director. We were the proud possessors of a video-recorder and she intended to hand the historic event on to posterity. She was going to create something ranking among the great cinema-tographic accomplishments of the age. She would film the reconstruction of the roof from every direction and angle, and in every climatic mood. She would capture with her zoom facility every dramatic detail and each focused frown on the faces of the men deeply engrossed in their work. The only exception here would be Martin, of course, who would supply smiling concentration.

She began by wandering nonchalantly in the upper garden to obtain a discreet bird's eye view through the plum tree branches, unmindful of the fact that by late autumn they offer little cover without their leaves.

From there, she strolled down to the caravan and, pretending to film the garden, would casually swing the camera round to the men. She ambled down the side of the house, ostensibly pointing at the windows, tilting the lens up whenever anyone showed his face over the roof edge.

125

The operational centre was the caravan, which she regarded as the best tactical place from which to make her forays. Equipped with the camera slung round her neck, her motives soon became transparent. She was fooling no one as she went in and out with the regularity of a nesting bird, or one of those figures in a chiming Swiss clock.

I am not sure who was the first to suspect something, but the men began to nudge each other in a self-conscious way and mutter out of the sides of their mouths. Their initial reaction was to position their photogenic sides to the camera and to adopt a kind of intense preoccupation with their work. But as the photo-call began to pall, they began to spice their reaction up with leers and grimaces and occasionally pointedly presenting their rear ends to the lens. My wife did not feel that this was in keeping with the high art form she was aiming for, and realising by now that her cover was blown, asked them to ignore her and adopt natural attitudes. Now I do not know how many would agree, but I am of the opinion that as soon as you ask someone to be natural, you elicit an amazing range of unimaginably grotesque poses. An intense desire to capture the quintessential self takes them over, and imposes grimaces and self-conscious half-smiles that end up making them completely unrecognisable.

Not only did the men's faces change, but their movements took on a consciously rhythmic regularity, as if they were all performing a mime. Whether this was by design, or something had set itself in motion subconsciously, it was difficult to say, but Martin started to shout orders at everyone as if he were drilling a squad on the parade square. Whenever he wanted more wood aloft, he would shout out, 'Wood chucking on the double!' When he needed mortar to bed the beams, it would be 'Bucket, Roger! Chop, chop!' The acceleration increased until he had got the men to move like the Keystone Cops in a Mack Sennett comedy.

Using my wife's surreptitious and haunting film making to advantage, whenever he sighted her behind bushes or sneaking around corners, he would shout out, 'Right lads, she's on to us

126

from the west side! Make yourselves look good for the camera!' and they would all be galvanised into motivated action.

I have to say Martin and his crew did a very good job in the end, and it was worth it not only for the finished product, but for the experience itself.

On the last day, just before the last tile had been laid, our carpenter friend came by and insisted on doing a Fiddler on the Roof dance to celebrate! He was joined by Martin and the others, in a chorus of 'If I were a rich man'.

I watched from below, thinking that Martin would certainly be richer. On reflection, I thought I was too. In addition, my wife has footage to die for.

16

Invaders

We were so involved with renovating our house that it had not occurred to us that other Brits were doing the same.

One day Pierre told us about the new *Anglais*, Don and Linda, who lived up the hill outside the village. Pierre was impressed that an English carpenter should want to bring his family of two young boys to settle in the Charente and have them educated in French schools. As a tradesman himself, Pierre admired even more Don's bravery in attempting to start a one-man business in a tax system that is extremely hostile to such ambition.

Before he came to the Charente, Don had been part of a maintenance team in an American forces camp in Germany, having upped and left his small terraced house in the north-west of England to seek opportunities in the newly opened European marketplace. He was right to finally put his roots down in the Charente because, although finding work was initially problematic, the increasing number of Brits buying property in the region soon opened up a demand for his services he could not have foreseen.

We had overheard whispers among the locals about this influx, but we were not aware of the extent of it. As pioneers in the area, we were not even sure that it could be right for them to settle there without first notifying us. As I said to my woman, 'Thar ain't nuthin' sacred any moe. Here we is, with ar fence-posts dug deep. We done claimed our plot o' lan' and, nex blink o' th'eye, yi got orl them proberdy-hungry varmints runnin' amuck jes' about ever'whar.'

The French farmers were delighted by the sudden interest taken by foreigners in their surplus old farmhouses that had been on the market for ages. There was little prospect of their being sold to the indigenous population: the only transaction had been for the purchase of land for agricultural purposes, and that was not too frequent.

The buildings, mostly inherited jointly by several members of the family, were falling derelict. Here was an opportunity for farmers to offload their old buildings to these invaders who were actually seeking to buy up what they had no further use for.

At first they sold their barns and farms at knock-down prices, but it was not long before many surrounding villages had at least one British family ensconced in their midst, whether it be for the holiday periods, for retirement, or, like Don and Linda, to settle and work there permanently. It got to the point where villages without foreign purchasers took it personally, and soul-searched for explanations as to why they were overlooked.

Once the demand was recognised, the prices inevitably rose and owners began to hold out for more, especially if the property in question had a splendid vista, or was well placed, by a river or lake, for example. Generally, the British were amazed by the amount of land that came with the properties, often forgetting that, although cheap to buy, it could be expensive to maintain.

My own concern was that the Charente should not become like the Dordogne, where the English had their own newspaper, and just enough French language to order two more brandies. Importing a chauvinist package for fear of losing identity is an intrusion in my view, not that I am criticising the English way of life (whichever one of the many kinds one might mean). In my humble opinion, it just does not root itself well in French soil. (Though one does hear of English people teaching the French to play cricket!)

Pierre and Danielle had already made friends with Don and

Linda and declared them 'personae grata'. They recommended us to visit them, and apparently had warned them to expect us to turn up. Expected we must have been, for on the day we knocked on their door, Don had arranged a particular welcome.

He opened the door, took one look, and in the time it takes to spit, said in his broad Lancashire accent, 'I know who you are.' Then pointing his finger at us in a business like way, he added, 'Right. Hold on a minute.' Turning indoors, he shouted out, 'Jimmy, they're 'ere! Come on, let's be 'avin' yer!' A stocky four-year-old boy suddenly appeared between his father's legs, shyly peering out and obstinately refusing to return our smiles.

'Now then, Jimmy, this is Mr Danby, the hactor from England – the one we've been expectin'. Righto! Are you ready, then? Go on, give it your best go.'

He thrust his small son forward to the front of the step. Jimmy, taking his cue, placed one hand on his hip, stared fixedly ahead and, with a deep and intense frown, delivered the phrase, 'In a handbag.'

'There you go!' said his proud father. 'As 'e got the part then? 'E's a bobby dazzler, an' no mistake, in't 'e?'

Although he would never have been a contest for Dame Edith Evans, I told young Jimmy he was up for the part next time I produced a dwarf version of The Importance of Being Earnest. He seemed pleased with that, though it was hard to say why.

'Oh, 'e's earnest, all right, aren't you, Jimmy?' interjected Don, beaming down at his offspring, before adding, 'But he doesn't come cheap, 'cos 'e's talented, see?'

I soon got the hang of Don's sense of humour, which plays off a pretended ineptitude, recalling Stan's role in the Laurel and Hardy films.

Jimmy was made the straight man on another occasion. I had devised a notice to put in the toilet that read 'We are served by a septic tank, and so visitors are requested to kindly refrain from depositing anything in the pan other than the toilet paper provided.'

Don had seen this pretentious-sounding notice pinned to the wall above the cistern, and when Jimmy returned to the living room, having just completed a major job in the cubicle, Don asked him what he had been doing there. Jimmy shrugged and said nothing.

'You didn't drop anything down the pan, did you?'

Jimmy seemed a little confused, and hesitated for a moment. Don wore an expression of deep concern at this point.

'Hey, Jimmy, you didn't drop anything but paper in the pan, did you?'

Poor Jimmy remained silent.

'Aw, don't tell me you went and did a job in there, did you?'

Jimmy nodded with timid uncertainty.

'Didn't you read the notice, Jimmy? Nuthin' else to be dropped down the pan but paper! That's wot it says.' Don shook his head sadly. 'Well, you'd better apologise to Mr Danby straight away fer usin' the toilet for illicit purposes.'

He turned to me and suddenly I was forced to be an Ernie Wise to his Eric Morecambe as he continued, 'I mean, Mr Danby, 'ere made it absolutely plain. Nuthin' other than paper means nuthin' but paper. I rest my case.'

I put Jimmy's mind at ease by assuring him that any time he wanted to perform his necessary toilet functions, he was free to do so. Don and his family looked on with grinning satisfaction as I was obliged to dot my 'i's and cross my 't's, explaining to Jimmy that the paper came after the performance.

When I had finished, Don said in heavy emphasis, 'Well, if only Mr Danby had made that clear in the first place, you could have sat in there without a care. Now I know it's permitted, I think I'll 'ave a go myself.' And he left the room with a determined expression.

Another episode was entirely within the compass of a Laurel and Hardy film. It began when Jimmy brought home a note from school to say he had won a pig in a lottery. The farmer who had donated the prize would provide the animal dead or alive, but it was entirely the lucky winner's responsibility to make his own arrangements thereafter. If alive, the winner would have to furnish it with accommodation, and if dead, he would be responsible for carving it up into manageable portions.

Don realised there was too much pig to squeeze in his freezer, so he agreed to sell half to a neighbour, the price to be determined by weight. The neighbour suggested they pick the live pig up in his lorry and then drive to a transport weighbridge. The intention was to weigh the lorry loaded with the pig, then take the pig off and weigh the lorry again. The weight of the pig would then be calculated by subtracting the unloaded from the loaded weight.

If you were to ask me why they couldn't just weigh the pig by itself and have done with it, I would guess that it wasn't heavy enough to register on the weighbridge. If you were to ask me why they didn't kill the pig, portion it and weigh the various cuts as they were made, I would have to guess I have not the faintest idea. But, how would a Laurel and Hardy film ever have been made if we wanted this kind of rational explanation?

Nothing conforms to your ideal result, and this exercise would be no exception. As soon as the whole process had been completed, Don made his calculation but, just from looking at the well-appointed beast, concluded that there was a gross under-estimation. He was convinced there must be something wrong with the weighbridge mechanism. The neighbour thought not, but after some arm-waving discussion, agreed to repeat the process.

For the second time, the pig was sent up the ramp onto the lorry, the combined weight recorded, the pig driven down the ramp, and the lorry minus pig weighed again. This time the calculated weight by subtraction greatly exceeded the first one, and Don was pleased to accept it. Not too surprisingly, with more arm waving and huffing and puffing, his neighbour thought the weight grossly overestimated.

Of course, once you have such a large discrepancy, it is

impossible to accept one calculation over another, and so Don was forced to concede that it was only proper to weigh the pig a third time and see if the result accorded with either of the previous. Accordingly, the pig was trotted up the ramp again – and so forth.

I wonder if the reader is already ahead of the story's end? In the best tradition of Mack Sennett, the third weigh-in equated with neither of the previous results, but fell somewhere in between. Don saw it as unfairly advantaging his neighbour and the neighbour considered it as biased in favour of Don. They began to get a little tetchy and Don suggested that, with all this trotting up and down the ramp, the pig was fast losing weight anyway. The neighbour suggested that whatever the pig's real weight, it bore little relation to the recorded weight, and that the problem could have been avoided if the initial result had been accepted. Don wondered if there was an ulterior motive for suggesting they got into this pantomime in the first place. They glared at each other for a while and then realised it was a stand-off.

After some silent scratching of heads, they came to the conclusion it was best to slaughter the beast first, and then come to agreement about price when it had been cut into manageable portions. This was satisfactory to all but the pig, of course, which was to be hung up and have its throat slit, not necessarily in that order.

They nearly broke into further dispute about whether the meat should be dressed before weighing, but Don, either from frustration or a sudden bout of generosity, decided to accept having it dressed, on the grounds that the pig was a perk, anyway. So it was resolved, and from that time on Don has bought all his meat from the hypermarket.

On one occasion, we had reason to be eternally grateful to Don – well, for a long time, anyway – on account of his dealings with one of Nature's unwelcome visitors to our house. We had already had intimate acquaintance with mice and voles, had been infested by hornets and had even had snakes curl round our toes while gardening in the autumn, but this was the first time we had been confronted by an impudent and demanding rat who took up residence in the house.

I must inform those who do not know, that rats can gnaw through mortar when they put their minds and teeth to it. Those who do know it embed broken glass into the mortar to deter such invasion. Being ignorant, I had omitted broken glass, and our particular rodent intruder managed to eat his way through the cement surround of the drainage outlet, and ensconced himself in the polystyrene behind the plaster right next to the shower.

As is the habit of ironic inevitability, guests were staying before we noticed the signs. Objects moved mysteriously during the night. First, a large bag of apples was rifled, and the contents scattered over the living room floor. A large mop head mysteriously travelled from beneath the sink to the shower room. Finally a whole loaf of bread was dragged from the kitchen to the toilet cubicle, only this time it was under the horrified eyes of a young woman visitor who was sleeping on the settee in the living room.

The bedrooms were immediately overcrowded with shivering females, exchanging their deep-seated phobias about sharing the residence with – of all creatures – urgh! – a RAT! It must be gigantic they said, in a mixture of horrified whispers and hysterical high-pitched shrieks.

'It was! It was!' shouted the witness.

From then on, it was almost impossible to inveigle our female guests downstairs at all.

The following night, everyone huddled together, listening for every slight noise below. The consensus was that it would be fatal to visit the toilet. The idea of a pair of eyes staring up at you as you sat in your most vulnerable position was more than they could cope with. A batch of makeshift potties was arranged, making the whole first floor look like a refugee camp.

135

In the morning, bleary-eyed, the guests peered fearfully round the banisters, searching for the latest signs of the beast's prodigious feats. Mythical powers were attributed to it. Something had to be done to rescue the situation; upstairs was becoming unbearably intimate.

Many diverse suggestions are thrown up when a problem of this sort arises, and the mind searches in many directions. The female guests recommended poison, preferring as they did that the rat went off to die in a decently quiet and invisible way. The male members of the group preferred to have it caught in a large trap that slammed down on its neck, thus allowing them to see the rat, and extend their arms wider each time they dramatised the anecdote. One tender-hearted girl made everyone smile by suggesting that we put down poisoned rat chocolate. Unlikely as it was, I found the stuff that same day, and, although it reminded me of the excesses of Lucretia Borgia, was desperate enough to buy it.

I laid down a whole choc bar that evening, only to find that Monsieur Le Rat turned his nose up at it. The following evening I left a mountain of poisoned grain, and this time was encouraged to find much had been consumed. Unfortunately this poison appeared to be meat to him, and he remained as active as ever. Someone told me later that rats have developed immunity to poisons.

My next move was to block the hole that led to his lair behind the plasterboard. I hoped, by this, to starve him to death if the poison did not first take effect. I blocked the hole with a miniature landslide of rocks, and consigned him to his fate. We heard him scrabbling behind the plaster, and I began to feel trapped, myself, as in a particular Edgar Allen Poe story where an incarcerated body becomes a presence preying on the conscience until madness takes over. The movements became feebler until silence set in, and everyone began to breathe more easily. I made myself very popular by saying that no creature could survive so much poison and then be denied food. We all felt better and winked, nodded and put our thumbs up at each other in growing confidence.

My wife decided it was time to begin a normal life again and went defiantly to luxuriate in a hot shower. The guests eagerly formed a queue to follow suit, until a scream rent the air, the like of which empties a dentist's waiting room. She exited ashen-faced from the washroom, loosely wrapped in a towel, as everyone backed away, fearful of catching something contagious. The cursed, death-defying, fabled monster rodent had evidently been prompted back to life by the warm water evacuated through the drainage pipes.

At this point, Don called round with a cunningly devised trap and a large wedge of Emmenthal cheese. Removing my rock landslide, he placed the cage charged with the cheese over the entrance, saying, 'These blighters are French, see. They don't recognise anythin' foreign.'

That night earnest prayers were said, and in the morning Don came round and proudly showed us the rat, well and truly trapped in the cage. It was a fine, healthy, if somewhat doleful, specimen that gazed out at us all. I felt elated enough to fall on Don's neck, but the guests were unable to share my enthusiasm. Indeed, the ladies refused to look at it, and the men, though curious to see the creature, confessed that it had taken much of the shine off their visit. They all left the next day, in a minor key, hardly looking better for the vacation.

Don took a snapshot of the rat in the cage, which still immortalises it. The memory is immortal, but the rat was drowned in Don's underground water cistern the same day.

We never again heard from our guests.

17

Remnants of War

I have often reflected on what life must have been like during the German occupation in the Second World War, and have carried with me around France a vague awareness of the feelings it left behind. It is an experience that divides us from the French, just as the Blitz of 1940 is something peculiar to us in Britain.

Our village in the Charente was next to the border designed to separate Free and Occupied France during the Second World War, and I noted at one point during the initial inspection of the house that a framed certificate had been pinned over the chimneypiece recording the owner's involvement in helping Jews to cross the border before Germany took over the whole of France.

If the subject of the occupation is ever broached in conversation, you get the impression that the French are brushing it aside with a, '*C'est la vie!*' But the Charentais who are old enough to remember, use this phrase with an earnest expression, and, in some cases, with emotion. They may well be saying, 'Life is like that,' but they are also implying that they wished to heaven it weren't. Much depends on their age and their personal experiences during the war, of course, not to mention their resilience. But one senses that they prefer to push it to one side.

This fact of not wanting to remember made the relatively nearby village of Oradour-sur-Glaine rather a mystery to me, for it was, until recently, a national monument to an atrocity perpetrated there

139

by the Germans in 1944, a few days after the Allies invaded Normandy.

On 10th June a German battalion entered the village and slaughtered the whole population: 642 people in all, including men, women and children.

There are theories as to why they did this, which we need not go into here, but I became curious to learn what the French Cultural Heritage Institute wanted the visitor to experience.

Oradour is in the Limousin, but no more than a half-hour journey beyond the boundaries of the Charente. The entrance to the main street, down which a local train once rolled on sunken rails, is now straddled by a set of tall gates. There was no fee to visit, but at the side of the gate stood a kiosk that sold brochures with lurid red pictures of scowling German soldiers menacingly waving bayonets. I bought one of these, and a postcard photograph, which had been retouched with unreal pastel colours, depicting the main street before the war. In it, the inhabitants stand on their doorsteps, all looking towards the camera in obediently stiff pose, presenting themselves as mute propaganda from the past. Their faded, almost cartoon forms stare out at us, insisting their innocence, and entreating us to recognise their undeserved fate.

I looked up from the card, and surveyed the village. It also challenged me with its jagged remains. Every building is open to the elements; the exterior walls almost razed to the ground. A few charred window openings and the sad remnants of fireplaces remain to speak of former lives. Ivy climbs over everything, including rusty bicycle frames that lean against interior walls, and sparrows' nests stick out untidily from niches. One or two burned-out carcasses of cars stand untidily in the road – a notice informs us that one belonged to the local doctor. Here and there, plaques mark places where men were executed in groups of ten.

For all this frozen testimony, on the day I visited, the warm summer breeze and the chirruping sparrows insisted on life's continuation. The village declared its terrible events, but there were no ghosts left behind. Roofless remains, jagged outlines and rusted carcasses all bore witness to deeds past. But the living strolled in the sunlight, and cast moving shadows.

I looked at my postcard again, and wished I could be moved to more pity for the dead; they deserve something from the living, and I willed myself to give it. I thought of the vacuum that would be left, if my wife and children had been taken from me thus. However, something obstructed pity, and I discovered it to be anger – anger (wholly pointless in the end) at the mindless cruelty of it all.

Suddenly the village reminded me of a film set, and this removed me even further from the reality. A group of passing French teenagers burst into youthful mirth, and I wondered how they could laugh in such a place, scarred as it was by malice and death. I smouldered at their insensitivity until I remembered that youth takes life for granted, and often lacks the power to imagine finality. There was no laughter here for me, but I understood how, despite the village's visible remains, the passage of half a century had somehow eroded the significance of what had taken place.

We moved on to the church. A dark-suited guide led forty or fifty of us into the ruined edifice and silenced us with an imperious wave of his hand. Having got our undivided attention, he gestured to us to form a wide arc, and began, a well-dressed messenger from a Greek tragedy, his rehearsed recitation of the dreadful narrative.

He told us that all the women and children were herded into this building and incinerated, as the Germans trained flame-throwers on them. He pointed to one corner and spoke of a crouching mother holding her young children to her breast; indicated the windows where panic-stricken women had scrabbled at the ledges only to fall to the floor as the machine-gunners strafed the building. He emphasised the futility of escaping, save (and here he raised a finger in a dramatic pause to get our focus) for one woman who lived to tell the tale. She managed to escape through a window, drop into the shrubbery and remain undetected until the last shot was fired. The guide's voice swelled and faded in peaks and troughs of emotion, and descended into a rallentando finale, his chin dropped on his breast.

I think everyone was more chastened than awed. For me, something was missing. It was a performance striving for tragedy that wasn't there. The revengeful cause that tragedy demands for the noble and great to be struck down was denied. This was just mindless barbarism enacted on the anonymous. Beyond stating the facts, there is just nothing to say about it. Better to leave the visitor to wander alone and come to terms with it as he may.

Yet, I cannot discount it, for it left its impression. There must be some reason to tell the story and preserve the village as a monument. I wonder, in any case, what the alternative would be? Would it be right to obliterate the village altogether? Should another village be built on its foundations? Or would that be an indecent cover-up?

Since our visit, the French have taken away its National Monument status, and the unattended village is left to the elements to be worn away. International relations demand it. I am not sorry, but I will remember the dreadful episode more for having been there.

I mentioned to Jeannine that we had visited Oradour the day after. She held me in her gaze for a second.

'*C'est dommage.*' What a pity,' she said, without expression. She turned without another word and went through her gate.

Whether she was referring to the village, or the fact that we had gone there, I knew she was escaping.

A week later, we invited Jeannine to afternoon tea in the garden. She turned up with biscuits as her contribution. It was never any good remonstrating with her; it only promoted huffing, puffing, arm waves and shrugging. She liked English tea, and had often taken it when she had worked in Paris. I showed her how to crook your little finger as you lifted the cup, which confirmed her in her worst suspicions of the English.

As we sipped our tea in this genteel fashion, she looked down over the village and said, out of the blue, 'My whole life is written on this village. The village is part of me.'

It was a moment to keep silent and pay close attention. She stopped to form something in her head before she said, simply, 'I can look at the whole village from here and it tells a story.'

I thought the slightest sound might break the brittleness of her thoughts. She faltered at first, and screwed her face into an apologetic frown, as if unsure it was right to speak about herself. I gave the slightest hint of a nod, which she took as permission.

'I was fifteen when the Germans came in 1940, you know. The village brought me up. I didn't know who my father was, and my mother didn't care. She let others look after me while she went off with men. I lived with the family who lived where I am now. They were kind, and gave me a home. They had a son, Henri, and we became very attached. He was called up into the navy, until France surrendered. Then all the young men made a dash for home, and tried to pretend they had taken no part in the war, in case the Germans took reprisals. Henri had to keep low. We were next to the frontier, so were not allowed out after dark. But we went anyway, because you could not be seen. I used to ride back and forth over the border on a bike, even during the day. The guards would look at my papers and search my satchel, but they never looked in my handle bars. That was how the Maquis got their messages through.' She giggled, remembering this as a childish pleasure.

'Sometimes I would come back late, and the guards would tell me off. After I did this a few times they got suspicious. They didn't find anything, but they put me in prison for a week with practically no food, to teach me a lesson.'

She shrugged and smiled, adding quickly, 'Well they had to, because the resistance was very active around here.'

'Were you a member of the Maquis?' I asked, drawn into the world of danger and excitement she described. She laughed.

'No. I never knew what they had put in the handlebars. At first they just told me to ride through the frontier post and leave the bike with some friends for a quarter of an hour. I liked doing it, because they would give me sandwiches and lemonade. But it was obvious what they were doing. In the end they let me in on it all. They swore me to secrecy and ordered me never to look inside the handlebars. They said that what I didn't know, I couldn't give away.'

'You make it sound fun,' I said, believing, from her expression, that she was sharing an invigorating memory. She looked at me as if she could not understand how I could conclude that. She sighed and said, 'Not really.'

She meditated for a moment, readjusting the perspective of her story. 'It gave us something to talk about. If we got back at the Germans in some way or other, we felt we were alive. But it wasn't fun. Nothing was fun.'

Her mood shifted as she entered a painful place. She looked at my wife and me in turn, before saying, 'They sent him to Poland, you know. Working in an ammunition factory, without enough to eat.' She nodded us into comprehension. 'We married, Henri and I. But soon after, they took him and sent him off with all the other young men of the village.'

We waited while she took a sip of her tea.

'One day, I got a letter from Henri. He wrote that he was exhausted and hungry. It was a terrible letter. At the end of it he said he did not expect to survive long, and wanted me to visit him. It was very difficult to get permission to travel anywhere. Poland was a very long way away. But I went to the German Commandant responsible for giving permits, and he said I could go if my mother would sign her consent. I said I didn't know where she was, or whom she was living with at that time. He insisted, "You have to find her and get her permission, because you're underage." I was married, but at sixteen I still had to have my mother's consent.' She smiled at the irony. 'I asked around the village and someone said she was living with a man in the next village. I told the Commandant, and he agreed to visit her and see if she would sign the paper. He was a good man, that German; he had a good heart. Well, he went to her and asked if she would let me go. She said she didn't care where I went, and if it was Poland, it was all the same to her. The Commandant came back with the signed papers, and said he was sorry for me – he was glad he didn't have a mother like mine.' She wore a stoic but rueful smile as she continued, 'Can you imagine how I felt when a German officer could say that about my mother?'

I wondered at the unimpassioned way she put this. It wasn't pity she sought; she was asking a question relevant to all of us. Our response would ultimately determine society. We said nothing.

'So I went to Poland. Henri was very ill when I saw him. But I was able to be with him and look after him for a week. It nearly broke my heart to leave him; he looked so frail. As I left him, he said he did not expect to see me again.' She paused. When she continued, it was as if she were accusing life itself.

'When I arrived back home I discovered that I was pregnant. The letters stopped coming. He was right. I never did see him again. He died without ever knowing that he had a daughter.'

She gathered her resources and put brightness back into her voice. She went on to tell us of her second husband, who bought the house from Henri's family, how she subsequently had two more children with him, and how, together, they had brought up all three offspring, until her husband's early death.

'And so, you see, I have had my sadness.'

145

Tea was over, and as we rose from the table I was aware of the incongruity of such a story in a garden full of sunny light. Throughout it I had responded with murmured grunts, afraid of appearing sentimental. She thanked us for the invitation and left.

As she went through the gate, I remembered her curt reply the week before. She had taught me, with simple candour, something that Oradour could not; personal suffering, simply told, digs deeper into the well of tragedy than collective events dramatically presented. Maybe, the telling of it is a stitch in the wound.

18

Gripes and Grapes

You can always get a move on in France, but you will never be able to compete with the French. They are so expert that, as you cruise along their roads well in excess of the speed limit, they make you appear to be dawdling.

If I have to put my foot down on the accelerator, it is usually because I am late for something; the average Frenchman stands on his pedals simply to pass the car in front. It is a compulsion with him. If he were driving a Citroen CV2 behind someone attempting the world speed record on the Nevada Salt Flats, he would have to try to overtake.

Of course, France has lots of straight roads left behind by the Romans, and these are a great temptation to open up the throttle. But this propensity for speed probably has a lot to do with coming into the modern world on the tails of the British. They learned a great deal from our mistakes during the Industrial Revolution, and have now overtaken us in manufacturing production, the creation of efficient railways, and in their network of cost-effective autoroutes.

They have their own set of unwritten rules of the road calculated to serve the racing driver mentality, which all British motorists should be aware of. If, for instance, you are waiting to emerge onto a main road, you are expected to wait patiently while the very long file of traffic speeds past, even if there is a gap of a quarter mile between any of them. You must not expect anyone to slow down and give a courteous flash of the headlights to allow you entry into the racing traffic, however long the file may be.

Of course, by the same token, if you are the only driver speeding down a major road a quarter of a mile away from someone waiting to get onto it, you can expect them to wait for you to pass before they attempt to get into your slip-stream. They are preserving the right of every fellow driver to fly along like a bat out of hell, and are affording others what they expect themselves. Any such recorded law would read: 'Drivers wishing to enter on to a main road must wait with monumental patience to allow traffic coming from either direction to cross their path, and respect all competitive racing and reckless overtaking at all times.'

When occasional impatience takes precedence, inevitable consequences follow. French road accident statistics are frightening. Whenever I travel down the Route Nationale 10, I notice the ever-growing number of flat, black, humanoid cut-outs on the side of the road marking the latest anonymous fatalities. They look like targets at SAS training camps, or suggest oversized figures for a giant macabre board game. Ineffectual notices begging drivers to cut down this senseless waste of life accompany them from time to time, but such supplications to preserve life have little effect on a lemming mentality. Even as I write, I hear on the radio of an accident involving multiple deaths on the RN10.

When the French crash their cars, they do so in spectacular style. The word 'accident' is synonymous with 'write-off', descriptive of both vehicle and occupants. They do not play around at denting each other's bumpers or panels; they go for the macho head-on Russian roulette, in significantly breakneck style. It is a sad, relentless price to pay for gratuitous speed.

The memory of one monumental folly remains embedded in my mind for ever. It is an incident that challenges credulity, and elicits crooked smiles from many who know I am espoused to the fictitious. It is absolutely true, honest, Guv!

148

Some years ago a car pulling a caravan, and thus a larger version of the 'bat out of hell', sped up behind us on the 'RN Southern Invitation to Disaster' (my name for it). Having flashed me into abject submission, it flew past on the fast lane towards a monster lorry and trailer travelling in the same direction. The driver of the caravan outfit began to draw up to the side of the high-sided trailer to overtake, just as curved arrows on the road began to indicate that a single-lane section was imminent. It was a case of pulling back and staying for some time behind the lorry or getting past the monster before the single lane began.

The gauntlet had been thrown down; the foot was pressed down hard on the throttle. As the caravan grew level with the high-sided bulk of the lorry, it began to oscillate, affected by the lateral force of the slip-stream. The next second it began to shake like a dog climbing out of the water just as the road was narrowing. The few remaining seconds to overtake were fast giving out, and it was clear that the senseless manoeuvre had to be abandoned.

The driver made the mistake of slamming on his brakes to pull back. As he did so, the caravan swayed heavily to the right, causing it to slew round and jack-knife so perfectly that it pulled the car round a hundred and eighty degrees to face the way it had come, like a toy some giant child had turned on his play mat.

The lorry thundered on with impunity and in blind ignorance, and we passed in the slow lane with just enough time to observe the dazed unbelief on the face of the driver and the manic rigidity of his posture, as he directly faced the oncoming traffic.

We never knew how, or even if, he managed to turn to face the right way, what state his suspension ended up in, nor what inconvenience he must have caused the cursing drivers of the following traffic. It was a miracle the caravan had somehow avoided hitting the lorry as it swung round. It was as if the Keystone Cops had taken part in the chariot race in Ben Hur. Cecil B. de Mille would have called it a wrap and hugged himself to death had he managed to get a stunt like that in the can.

Later that day, reflecting on the affair, the knuckles of my hand holding the glass of Cognac tightened involuntary and the throat contracted as I swallowed the nerve-steadying elixir. It's an amazing thing that at moments of imminent danger, adrenaline takes you past the related fear. The full realisation that you and your family might have been wiped out, if the barmy caravaner's outfit had swung into your lane, comes later. Just thinking about it now has caused me to involuntarily pour another two fingers of Cognac.

At such times you appreciate just what special properties Cognac can bring to your life, and so I always make sure I have an adequate supply. This calls for frequent visits to a distiller in deep, dark vineyard territory. He is unknown to many imbibers of the liqueur. But to those who have learned of his secret location, he offers generous discounts. I say no more than that, but I wink my eye, tap my nose in street-wise fashion and seal my lips.

A visit to my friend, the distiller (anyone prepared to give such good discounts has to be a friend) is a strange experience to the novice. You drive into a small courtyard off a side-road in a small village and walk over to a door glazed with dark one-way glass panes, ring a bell and wait patiently until the door is opened a hand's width. A low, insinuating languorous voice says, '*Oui*?' and a heavy-lidded eye travels over the assembled visitors.

'We were told by Monsieur X that you sell liquid refreshment to the passing traveller. Is that right?'

If Monsieur the Distiller has made his appraisal and finds you acceptable to his scrutiny, he opens the door wide and beckons you in with a pale, mysterious smile. It must have been like that when standing in front of the sliding door grille of a speakeasy during the American prohibition.

Having gained access to the small entrance hall, you peer into the dark passage beyond and can make out another group of 'passing travellers' tilting back glasses of amber nectar, next to a tiny bar set beneath three immense barrels. Disproportionate laughter explodes whenever anyone says anything the least bit amusing, and this is followed immediately by ruminative silences, making it sound like canned laughter in a TV comedy. The liquid is being rolled round the palate, so that proper judgement can be made, or at least the imbibers can give a faint impression of being connoisseurs.

Quiet expressions of ruminative appreciation, the nodded head, the pursed lips and gently fluttered eyelids are the going rate for entrance into this select society.

You take note and hope to make a good impression when your turn comes. Your turn comes after the silky-voiced patron has submitted you to a pantomimic introduction. You are asked to stand in front of two mirrors, one convex and the other concave. The first renders an elongated, emaciated image of yourself, a life-size version of Lowry's matchstick men; the second the bow-legged, robust, stocky dwarf version that aggressively thrusts its belly forward.

'Een the first mirror, you can see 'ow great is your need of the beverage that I am going to offer you. Een the second wan you can see 'ow eet 'as refreshed you and geevs you new strength. Eet 'as feeled you out. You are a new man.'

You would vehemently deny ever having seen the creature in the mirror, so perhaps he is right. This grotesquely belligerent dwarf is not, in anyone's imagination, going to encourage greater consumption; the helpless giggles and appreciative grunts down the passage make you impatient to get to the business of the day. But you are aware that your appreciation of his heavy humour is also part of the deal. You laugh and point at yourself and cavort and bend backwards to accentuate the distortion, while the host looks on with an implacable expression that seems to size you up as an absolute idiot. You tell yourself it is worth it, and, anyway, isn't humility good for the soul?

You are finally taken to join the other revellers, already greatly strengthened by Monsieur the Distiller's generous helpings. He could pass for a troll in Lord Of The Rings himself, with his large round head set on his squat body, watching with undemonstrative pleasure his clientele performing for him.

He washes some glasses in a bucket of cognac filled with the residue from glasses of previous pie-eyed visitors, who somehow forgot to finish their drinks. Monsieur asks you what you would like to try first; six-year-old Cognac, twenty-year-old Cognac, or Pineau des Charentes, a carefully blended composition of Cognac and grape juice.

Does it really matter, since you are going to try all three, anyway? Yes, it does. Monsieur will get the measure of you on the strength of your choice.

You will be thought a bit of a barbarian if you do not take the twenty-year-old Cognac while you are still sober enough to appreciate its qualities. First it must be inhaled deeply, but not too swiftly, to prepare the nasal cavities to receive the vapour from the imbibed liquid. It must be savoured with an uncontaminated palate, he tells you. The liqueur must slide under the tongue and round the oral pockets before descending the virgin throat.

Well, you go along with this poetic nonsense for the sake of taking away the stuff at a very reasonable price. You also let Monsieur suspend your nose over one bunghole of the barrel while he blows vapour up it from another.

To all the English visitors he has the same story to tell, which is that he is seeking to marry an Anglo-Saxon virgin, who will bear him children to carry on the family name and the business. He says this with a twinkle, but, in fact, his name on the bottles will disappear with him, unless he can become a legal parent.

I ask him why he wants an Anglo-Saxon virgin, and he tells me that he does not believe there are any French ones left. I leave it there, not being qualified to make valid comparisons.

'You weel 'elp me find wan, yes?'

'Yes, of course. We'll search diligently.'

He nods enthusiastically, gives you a disbelieving smile and asks someone in the party to place their mouths under one of the barrel taps set high on a shelf. There is usually some simpleton with sufficient alcohol already coursing round his or her veins to take up the invitation, with the inevitable consequence of having a river trickling down the chin and onto the chest or bosom region. I never believe that this comes as a surprise; how could it?

The gay-abandoned group is now led on a small tour into an adjoining cellar beyond sliding doors. This is for the purpose of allowing us a brief tantalising smell of the Pineau des Charentes that he retains for his own use in a huge oak cask, which stands next to the twenty-year-old Cognac.

Having whetted our appetites to no good purpose, he invites a carefully chosen female member of the party to climb a ladder leaning against this vat, armed with a small scoop, to help herself to the liquid contents therein. The lady leans over the rim and, as she takes a sample, reveals to all and sundry a generous view of her knickers.

No one says a word, except Monsieur who tells the lady that she has seen what no one else can see, and hopes she thought the taste of the Pineau was worth the climb. She nods vigorously. The distiller smiles and shrugs and asks everyone if they are enjoying the tour, before leading the grinning group up a tower overlooking the whole of his domain. He tells us of happier days when Portuguese peasants used to come every year to help gather the grapes, and slept on rows of truckle beds.

Now, he adds, in a sad, insinuating tone, 'I 'ave to sleep alone while ze grapes are boiled and ze vapour is collected in ze copper.' We shake our heads and try to show some semblance of sympathy. Someone giggles until his languid stare ominously settles on them.

At last, we return to the tasting area and put our orders in. Some of the party ahead of us have brought five-litre demijohns and have them filled with the best Cognac available to carry away on two-wheeled trucks.

One chap, a Canadian, produces a book listing all the best growers in the Charente, and points to a page devoted to Monsieur the Distiller's brew. We make appropriately impressed noises and order five bottles of Pineau and two of the twenty-year-old Cognac. Monsieur the Distiller makes a heavy point of telling you what it would cost you if you bought the Cognac on the open market, and then with the confident Mafia smile of one with an offer you cannot refuse, tells you the risible cost when you pay him cash.

With a mixture of elation and guilt, you leave, and tell him you will be back soon. At that price he knows you will.

'Of course,' he says, 'You weel tell your friends, and they weel come and taste, too, yes?'

'They most certainly will.'

'An' you weel reemambour the English virgin?'

'We'll get a search party on it, straightaway!'

I drive very slowly all the way home.

Before we found our 'friend', we used to visit the large Cognac houses in the town of Cognac itself, and they certainly put on a good show. They are too posh to show anyone's knickers, but they have high technology for their presentation. When we visited Hennessey it was Peter Ustinov's urbane voice that provided the commentary for their film. But it is a much more restrained experience than the one offered by our friend, the seeker of virginity.

People standing in the waiting room before the Hennessey tour tend to speak in whispers associated with doctors' waiting rooms. Even Dutch visitors, whose loud exchanges always make me think they are going to spit on the floor any minute, speak with uncharacteristic restraint. The Americans slouch and look a little bored, as though they know they are not going to be the least bit impressed by anything; it's all bigger back home. One tall middle-aged American guy, smoking a cigar, looks as if about to buy the place up, lock, stock and barrel, but the tour guide, probably an English student working during her holidays, promptly tells him that smoking is not permitted because of the flammable fumes everywhere. He stubs it out on a large tray and suddenly looks less confident.

The few French visitors, most of whom probably prefer whiskey, seem more relaxed and animated. I wish I could emulate them. I have tried to look French on a number of occasions. This involves extravagant shrugging, and arms raised to heaven, pouting the lips and shaking the head while saying, '*Bah oui*,' and even grimacing and splaying the arms as if addressing a crowd over Caesar's body.

All to no avail; it convinces no one – not even if I wear a beret. Leaving aside my unconvincing French, I think I must walk with an English accent, or something.

One group of visitors that gave me the greatest pleasure during one of these tours was a bus-load of Japanese who arrived late. The Japanese courier bowed to the tour guide and said, 'Solly we alive rate. We are or leady to rissen attentively flom this time. Prease to commence the tour.'

The whole group of Japanese tourists nodded and bowed as if taking a curtain call at a performance of The Mikado, and the ladies made subdued giggling noises.

The tour was comprehensive. We viewed vats, gazed at grape presses, dwelt on distilleries and mused on mysteries, peering through cobwebbed panes into the dark store rooms called *Paradis*, and full of the best Cognac from previous years. This, we are told, is preserved to blend with the product of less favoured harvests, so that the overall quality of the product can be maintained. The family name rests on the success of this blending and a chief blender is paid a fortune on account of his 'nose' that determines the quality of each harvest. The nose is mysteriously inherited from father to son, and is insured for a sum comparable with Betty Grable's legs in the 1940s. What the nose knows, goes.

At each stage of the tour, the Japanese broke away from the rest of the assembly to take photographs, not of the exhibits, but of themselves. They ranged themselves round vats, barrels, bottling machinery, the onion-shaped distilling copper – even the film screen – with an efficiency that reminded me of rehearsals for a musical. They all seemed to know precisely where their chalk marks were and the ladies all giggled in concert, precisely on cue. When they returned home, their films would exclusively record smiling Japanese faces completely blocking out whatever they were supposed to have visited. They always appeared attentive, and their polite smiles lasted throughout the tour, even when the guide spoke of the dreadful outbreak of phylloxera in the middle of the nineteenth century.

'And where did it come from?' the guide asks.

We shrug our ignorance.

'America!'

We focus hard on the two Americans, who try to abrogate responsibility with a quick, 'Whad'ya know?'

The matriarch adds defensively, 'Tha's a heck of a long ways back.'

Most of the party were not convinced by this, and looked as if they were about to encourage them to get out their cheque-books and offer compensation. The Japanese continued to smile, having understood not a word throughout.

The guide surveyed the circle of Japanese shining teeth, searching for one look of sympathetic appreciation of the dreadful event. She looked at the Japanese courier, who remained impassive. She accepted defeat and told us it was the end of the tour and that we would be offered complimentary drinks of twenty-year-old Cognac in the reception hall, 'if you would like to accept.'

156

More to the point would have been, 'unless you have the willpower to refuse.'

We did not.

We wrote, 'What a lovely surprise!' in the visitors' book to mark what was probably our fifth visit, and emerged into the blinding sunlight, to describe a slightly less than direct line to the car, smiling at everything and nothing. Which, as I drove home very carefully, I reflected is precisely what you should do after tasting this amber nectar.

19

Monsieur Hercule

Money is the root of all evil. Waiting for enough to get on with the work on a French house convinced me of it. However, one day I came across Monsieur Hercule, who became the means of speeding things up more than our wildest hopes imagined.

His sheer enjoyment in putting his back into a task is phenomenal, and the work does not need to be particularly creative to ensure his involvement. He is as willing and eager to dig out a whole drainage system as to build you a set of ornamental garden steps. His special skill lies in being able to do just about anything at all.

Having retired from full-time work, he is convinced that, if he were to refrain from physical exertion for a week, he would atrophy and be in his grave before he could receive his next social security payment. There is little danger of this happening, for his reputation goes before him by word of mouth from everyone who uses his services. Someone asks you if you know of anyone who could do some roof mending, tile laying, wall building, rendering, plastering, plumbing – you name it – and the first to come to mind is Monsieur Hercule.

I first discovered him up a ladder (which is to say, he was up the ladder and I was at the bottom). He was pointing a neighbour's wall, and I was struck by the care with which he worked, and the quality of the finish achieved in a relatively short time.

Having exchanged a few discreet words with the neighbour and discovered that Monsieur Hercule's hourly rate was attractively low, I approached him and asked if there was any chance he might do some work for me when he had finished working on the neighbour's house. He sized me up carefully, and after some musing conceded that perhaps it might be possible. I was no doubt being measured up as the kind of human being he would want to offer his services to. 'Measuring up' proved to be a demanding experience worth every strenuous effort.

Monsieur Hercule is built like a bear, and works with the same lumbering, inexorable pace of one. He brings to mind the self-contained but amicable version of a regimental sergeant-major, with his trim moustache, shining clean-shaven face and unquestioned authority.

If I were to imagine him in a battle scenario, it would be to see him clamber carelessly over the top of the defence lines and amble towards the enemy with unstoppable determination to finish the job with quiet efficiency. Merely armed with a shovel, he would give serious cause for concern to the other side.

Anyone employing Monsieur Hercule must know his rules. It is most important to state precisely what you want him to do. He does not like dithering about. If you are not certain, then he will tell you what you want, and you are then required to leave it to him to get on with it.

Another essential is to order all materials necessary for the job ahead of his arrival. Any deficiency in this respect is severely frowned on, and being frowned on by Monsieur Hercule is to feel oneself shrink into the earth.

Should you fall short in your duties, the best thing to do is look sheepish and smack the side of your face, while he shrugs his disappointment at your failings and tells you that it could result in his being paid for just hanging around doing nothing. You must immediately get in your car and race to the nearest builders' merchant to get the materials.

If, in the interests of cutting down the cost, you wish to assist him in the work, he offers no objection but you will not be permitted to take part in anything requiring real skill.

If you go ahead of him and partly complete what you wish him to finish, then you must be prepared for some scathing or pitying looks at the inferior quality of your attempt. He will give a cursory glance at your work, shrug, smile wanly, and emit sotto voce, '*bah!*'

If you ever get a '*Pas mal*,' from him it feels like an A+ for an essay on Plato. You will nevertheless receive a comprehensive list of all the things you should and should not have done. There is no grace in you, and you simply hang your head.

He never arrives on site later than seven o'clock in the morning, and begins work immediately. If you are going to be his assistant, then he will expect you punctually on site at the same time.

He simulates respect for his employer by saluting you in a jocular way with, '*Bonjour, Chef!*'

You return, '*Bonjour, Monsieur Hercule!*'

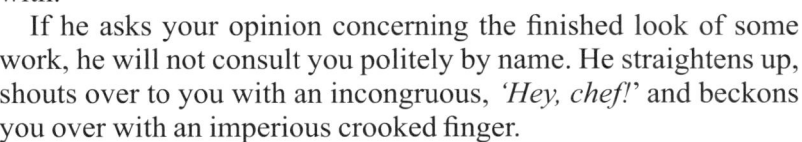

He asks you how *La Grande Chef* indoors is today. You say she is not up yet. He raises his eyes to heaven and shrugs with a philosophic smile. Immediately these formalities are completed, the work begins and your status as employer is wholly dispensed with.

If he asks your opinion concerning the finished look of some work, he will not consult you politely by name. He straightens up, shouts over to you with an incongruous, '*Hey, chef!*' and beckons you over with an imperious crooked finger.

I once tried some mild resistance to this by asking, 'You mean, right this minute?'

'*Bah, ouaie!*' he retorted an octave higher than usual, and I jumped to it with a promptness that surprised even me.

If he somehow convinces you that he thinks the customer has a right to have the job done their way, by all means state your preference, and then expect a hundred reasons to illustrate how your impractical suggestions will lead to catastrophe.

My wife took to making detailed drawings of what she wanted the finished project to look like. Leaving aside the abysmal lack of perspective, they were pretty accurate and understandable. She would slide these drawings in front of Monsieur Hercule in a deferential way and with a diffident smile ask him if he thought such a thing were possible. Such a question inevitably elicited an expansive and jocular, '*Mais, ouaie, bien sûr! Tout est possible!*'

Theoretically possible they may have been, but the drawings would never be fully realised.

Yet there was only one occasion on which my wife was disappointed, and then only temporarily. Monsieur Hercule was instructed (if that is the correct word) to build a set of steps from the base of the house to the lower garden. My wife had drawn the elevation and plan in some detail, specifying small steps with some stone surface peeping out through the rendering to give a rustic effect. He looked at the drawings and nodded wisely, convincing her of his compliance. She was confident enough to go off shopping for the day, leaving Monsieur Hercule to complete the work 'as per', as we say in the trade.

On returning home, she rushed to the site, where he was just about to complete the last touches to a magnificent flight of steps with curved treads and imprinted patterns. They were appropriate for any of Francois Premier's chateaux on the Loire. She stood wide-eyed and turning to me said,

'But ... they're nothing like my drawings!'

Monsieur Hercule stood ready to be praised for the magnificent work he had completed, and was confronted by my wife's face full of pain and confusion. A tear started to fall down her cheek.

'It's all different. Not what I wanted at all,' she said.

I have never been less grateful in my life to stand between two people incapable of speaking each other's language. Monsieur

Hercule, seeing my wife's response, looked at me for an explanation.

'She is overcome with joy,' I said. 'It is all too much for her.'

He beamed. My wife glimpsed his response, and asked, 'What does he find so amusing?'

'It is not amusement, my darling. It is his embarrassed way of showing his regret at having failed to provide what you wanted.'

'Well, you can tell him I am not pleased with the result, and that he will have to start all over again.'

She turned on her heel leaving Monsieur Hercule bereft of all expected compliments. He stared into my face again, as she left the scene, her body drooping with disappointment.

'She is overcome,' I said, with careful deliberation, 'and has to go and lie down. She cannot find the words to thank you. But you can see how moved she is.'

He nodded his profound understanding, and continued to smile with quiet self-satisfaction. We nodded in unison to register our knowledge of the female mind, like two toy dogs on the back shelves of cars, until I went to face the music with 'her indoors'.

After a day or two, she came round to accepting the steps, then to liking them, and, by the end of a week, to seeing them as a wonderful asset. Eventually, her emotional trauma having dissipated, she found the words to express her gratitude to him, freely translated, of course.

His part in the restoration of the old decrepit barn was epic but, at this point, I wish to place on record that it was I, and I alone, who laid the foundations and built the front and dividing internal walls without a single reproachful look from Monsieur Hercule. I crave a certificate to register the fact, and would display it over the threshold. I may have one made as soon as he is no longer around to see. Something like, 'These walls received the Monsieur Hercule Silent Approval Award.'

Beyond that, however, it was all downhill. At each attempt to contribute my DIY skills, I received a graphic description of the potential costly consequences of my ineptitude. I laid some drainage pipes that he informed me would eventually result in a monumental blockage.

Having smacked my face, I ask him if he can possibly remedy the situation?

'*Tout est possible!*' he says, and I nod with profound gratitude.

I had installed and fitted a shower cubicle. It will, he tells me as soon as he lays eyes on it, have to be disassembled and taken off its base to enable the walls to be properly rendered and replaced with sufficient height given for proper drainage.

Can he possibly …?

'*Tout est possible!*'

As the need for new skills arose, I would ask if he did plastering, plumbing, or electrical installation, to which he always responded with, '*Bah, ouaei!*' in a tone of amazement that I could ask such a question. Afraid of offending him, being considered a doubting Thomas, and taken off his list of acceptable clients, I stopped asking and left him to it. My 'faith' was invariably rewarded.

Great though his work was on the barn, his finest accomplishment, and the basis upon which I refer to him as our ministering angel, is his conversion of the *cave* into an unimaginably habitable room.

A lot of pondering had been given over to it. We had already put two windows in to make the gloomy interior seem a bit cheerier. This benefited the ferns no end. However much light one provided, damp remained the problem. We had spoken to several folk about the invasive stream, eliciting various wacky ideas. One friend suggested putting pillars on the ground, and laying joists across them to support a new floor. This ignored the fact that it would raise the floor to a level that would oblige me to walk with a permanent stoop. My wife thought this might be an attractive feature, reminding one of the stature of the average French peasant in the Middle Ages. Speaking as a six-footer, I suggested the medical bills for a back condition might outweigh the attraction. In any case, I made her accept that, even if we were not

164

actually sloshing about in silt, the damp would still rise up through the floorboards. We threw that idea out of the windows.

Her own romantic idea was to dig channels wherever we saw water seeping onto the floor, and then, having tiled all the dry areas, to cover the fern-covered stream beds with reinforced glass and light them up with waterproof lamps. She believes she remembers seeing such a thing at Lourdes at Bernadette's Fountain of the Virgin and finding it very attractive. I hardly thought our stream merited this attention, not having the same miraculous healing properties. She thought that was an unnecessary remark. I felt it was no more unnecessary than turning the floor into a miniature version of the sewers of Paris, and we spoke little for half a day.

We took Monsieur Hercule down there, and straight away he smiled his secret smile to show that such cellars held no fears for him.

Would it be possible ...?

'*Bah ouaei! Tout est possible!*'

He had seen and tamed many such *caves*. We were wide-eyed with anticipation to know how. He tapped his forehead and smiled the smile of a chess champion about to make his winning move.

'*Je commençerai demain.*'

I forget precisely how W.B. Yeats put it, but to paraphrase his lines: 'It was written on a leaf with the juice of a berry, And I laughed and cried because it was so simple.'

Only the insensitive will be able to hold back their tears as I explain as follows: The solution lay in a metre each of gravel, sand and mixed aggregate, twenty bags of cement, some drainage pipes and couplings and fifty breeze-blocks. The latter he used to front the back wall through which the water made its entrance, behind which there was a sloping culvert gathering the water and expelling it at one end. Then he laid the drainage pipes and directed all seepage to one exit point in the outer wall.

Over the whole system he directly shovelled the gravel. On this he laid a barely moist mix of concrete, strong enough to dry off before it could sink into the gravel. Finally he made a damp-resistant membrane of plastic covers, which happened to be lying around, and finished with a levelled coat of mortar ready to be tiled. The result caused my wife to weep with joy, and I have never seen Monsieur Hercule beam so brightly. Ardent DIY experts may find all that information useful one day; Ladies, I ask your indulgence.

Our joy was only minimally diminished when, having completed this miracle, he informed me of the imminent danger of the whole of the floor above collapsing.

For as long as we could remember, we had been conscious of bouncing across the floor, as the cups on the table gently clinked against each other. Clearly, this indicated that there was some give in the joists below. My wife had frequently expressed her concern that one day soon we would suddenly vanish in a pile of timber and rubble when the floor gave way. I countered her fears with a dismissive laugh, and reminded her that the house had stood there for centuries; proof that it would continue to do so for centuries more.

A bouncing floor, I said, was just another feature of the place to remind her of what life was really like for the average French peasant in the Middle Ages. She gave me a disdainful look and replied that when people do nothing about the ravages of time, they are eventually devoured by them.

It was not comfortable, then, to see her elation when her worst fears were confirmed by Monsieur Hercule. It took several days for me to recover from a sense of betrayal. Thereafter, I was treated to periodic subtle references to the need to take female intuition seriously.

'I just knew something was wrong,' she would murmur, loudly enough for me to catch. When we had guests, she voiced this phrase with gay confidence, making them turn to me with reproachful looks. How blind could I have been not to see the imminent danger? No, it was not an easy time at all.

Could Monsieur Hercule remedy the situation? What a

ridiculous question! He would place two perpendicular oak supports under the main beam to prevent it collapsing and then insert an additional set of cross-beams between the existing ones to prevent the floor bouncing.

'*Voilà! Tout est OK, et vous êtes tranquilles*,' he says with a conjurer's smile.

'Go ahead,' I said.

'As soon as possible, please,' said my wife.

'*Allez!*' said Monsieur Hercule. And off I went to the builders' merchant again.

Monsieur Hercule was on site the following morning at his usual ungodly hour, to drag us from sleep with the sound of sawing and hammering. As we sat at breakfast with our guests we felt decidedly guilty, having invited them for a week to escape the noisy bustle of London. Here they were subjected to clamorous activity directly above a construction site.

A break in work suddenly made us realise we were shouting at each other, and we lowered our voices and smiled sympathetically in a relieved way. But this relief was a cruelly short calm before the storm, and we were suddenly in a war zone. A six-pounder's explosive force jerked us up off our chairs, the first of a continuous bombardment.

We began to look as if we were travelling over an assault course for tanks. Our speech came in hiccups, as we attempted to spread butter and jam on crisp French bread, and drink the choppy waves of coffee that slapped over the rims of the cups. We were finally driven from our seats and made to rescue what we could from the debris on the table. As we filed into the courtyard, my wife apologised abjectly to our guests, who said they found it was all very 'interesting'.

By now, the floor was visibly dancing up and down at each explosive impact. In a tone implying little option, my wife asked me if it was possible I might have it in mind to ask Monsieur Hercule for an explanation of what was going on.

My courage has never been tested under fire, except against

167

bottles, and if we had not had guests, I might have asked her if she possibly had it in mind to go and use her feminine charm on him. But, in front of visitors, I find myself instinctively adopting the role of male protector.

I descended the steps, a brave front covering trepidation. Creeping down the last few steps, I peered into the *cave* to see Monsieur Hercule striking a massive oak upright with a huge mallet, like Mr Universe with his gong at the start of a Rank film. It took several of these blows to move the support a centimetre, and it was obvious that, even with his weight behind them, the job was going to take some considerable time.

He caught me peering in.

'Ah!' I said, swiftly. 'So … It's all going well, then?'

'*Ouaie.*'

'Quite a job, no doubt.'

'*Ouaie.*'

I nodded reflectively. He shrugged, waiting for me to say something intelligent.

'Right … So I'd better let you get on, then.'

'*Bah, ouaei!*' he said in his upper register.

Having been dismissed, I returned to the others in the courtyard. The explosions started up again.

'What did he have to say?' asked my wife.

'He is terribly sorry for the noise, but there is no way of getting the supports in place except by brute force. He said he will try to complete the job as soon as possible.'

'Amazing!' she exclaimed to the guests, 'He's never said that much in a week before!'

I shrugged, spread my hands out to 'rest my case' and kept silent.

There was no alternative but to go out for lunch and, with a hand over one ear and the phone pressed against the other, like a lieutenant in the trenches ringing down the line for reinforcements, I managed to book a table in a nearby village. We made the meal last a very long time and dawdled all the way home.

By this time, Monsieur Hercule had the supports in place and was in the process of inserting the cross-beams. This provided our guests with an additional topic for after-dinner conversation. The floorboards began to rise, as did the door-jamb dividing the two rooms. Cupboard doors opened one by one of their own accord, and furniture began to shift around as the joists were knocked into place. I compare the experience with that of standing on the moving platform in the Science Museum to feel the effect of an earthquake.

We retreated to the courtyard again and chatted above the noise. My wife told our guests how wonderful it would be to have a solid floor at last. I told them it would be wonderful to have a reasonably level one at the end of the day. She told them it never had been level. I agreed, but explained to them that the doors and cupboards were being pushed out of vertical to the floor, however level it was or wasn't. We would not be able to shut them, I added. She said it might remind us of how life was in the Middle Ages. I said that even in the Middle Ages people opened and closed doors. And so we passed the time agreeably until Monsieur Hercule came up the steps to stand over us and declare, with great satisfaction, that all had been completed.

I did mention the cupboard doors to him. He agreed, with an enthusiastic nod, that they would not close properly, but thought that, in time, things would settle down and with some trimming here and there, we might be able to force them into place.

What if we could not?

'*Bah, phuph!*' he muttered. And since this was all he was prepared to say on the matter, we thanked him and paid him. He drove off in his beat-up car with a cheery wave, shouting '*A bientôt, chef!*'

I sorted the door and cupbards with some clever sawing and planing. The tea-cups no longer rattle when we cross the room, but there is a hump in the floor.

However, Monsieur Hercule continues to work for us from time to time, and long may he do so. I have got used to being ordered about in such a good cause, and I would rather have someone with flair than someone who would take any suggestions I have seriously. I have little vision of what things will look like when finished. I need someone like Monsieur H. to tell me what I want or present me with a *fait accompli*, so that I can get on with the other things in my life.

Writing this book has been one of them.

20

Looking after the Leap

A landscape painter studies perspective before he begins his art; an actor researches a character before he attempts to portray it. I had no idea what the house would look like at the end, or where my nose would lead me. I learned most in hindsight, or, at best, during the process.

I am pleased by the idea of having rescued a sad, one-eyed tower and made of it a home that gazes confidently out over the valley. I like being able to say I was one of the very first to purchase a property in the Charente and can claim, in some part, to have led the way. But I sometimes look at the original photographs of the place and wonder what on earth urged me to make such a leap. When I sit on the terrace and survey the result, I am amazed at the help and support I mystically received from friends, and even strangers, who rescued me from my blunders.

There are so many relationships I would have been denied outside the Charente; an intimate bonding with my cement mixer, that faithfully swallowed as fast as I could feed it, and spewed its masticated contents to feed my voracious appetite for re-shaping the landscape; the brief but exciting acquaintance with mechanical diggers, invited to a garden party to gorge themselves on the hillside behind the barn and spew it out to make terraces; and my weekly appointments with my three trusty musketeers, hedge-cutter, chainsaw and hover-mower, sworn into service of the cause.

I would never have been handed the gift-wrapped ego-trip of directing a group of young French students in a self-devised summer *spectacle*. Their touching confidence in the direction of a middle-aged English guy with no CV to show, was testimony to their blind courage.

They rehearsed in a sloping meadow, slept in tents, and sat cross-legged on damp turf, to eat food cooked on an open fire and served on metal plates, gladly espousing the life of medieval strolling players. To complete the experience, they even took my advice to stage their entertainment in the middle of a football pitch under hastily rigged lights, rather than on the curtained stage of the village *Salle des Fêtes*.

Thereby hangs a tale not told here, but one that lives with me still.

There is one tale I will tell, finally, of a brief encounter that was the greatest undeserved blessing. It begins with a telephone call from a close friend, Sylvia. I pick up the receiver.

'Hullo?' I say.

'Trevor, you'll never believe this, but we've had a strange call from a Frenchman, asking if we know anyone called Trevor *Blah*.'

'I said, "We don't know a Trevor *Blah*. However, we do know another Trevor." So this Frenchman said, "Well, get him to ring us on my number."'

She gives me the number, and intrigued, I dial it.

'*Oui?*' says the voice at the other end. Our exchange is in French, but occasionally the man flexes a verbal muscle by inserting an English word.

I begin.

'I've been given this number by a friend, who got it from someone who asked her to contact me and ask me to ring this number.' (Sometimes my French sentences can get as elliptical as that.)

'Oo are you?' asks the voice, in a suspicious tone.

'I am Trevor Danby.'

'I do not know a Trevor Danby. Why are you ringing?'

'I don't know. I was told to ring someone who wanted to talk to Trevor.'

'You are not the Trevor I want to talk to.'

'Which Trevor do you want to talk to?'

'Eet ees not Trevor – what you say – Donbee?'

'Right. Well, I do have another name.'

'Another name?' asks the voice incredulously. 'Why 'ave you two names?' he continues, instantly alerted to the possibility of my criminal intentions.

'One I write under, and one I was born with.'

This does not satisfy the voice at all.

'What is your other name?'

'Blah,' I reply, feeling guilty already.

'Aaaa-ah!' (a pause to gather breath) 'But why 'ave you not say this? That is oo I am wanting to speak,' the voice says, expansively.

'That's good!' I respond, caught up in the sudden bonhomie, 'So, what can I do for you?'

'Ah, aah! But eet ees what can I do for yooo!' continues the voice, effusively, making me think it is going to try to sell me something.

'I'm afraid I have no idea what,' I reply, carefully.

'Ees there anything you are missing?' it asks.

'Oh, dear,' I think. 'What is the equivalent of double glazing in the Charente?'

'No doubt you will tell me,' I continue, holding my cynicism in check.

'A leetle something black, wizout which you weell be sad.'

I try to imagine what little black thing would make my life happier, and am about to put down the receiver on suspicion of being approached by a vendor of articles of a certain adult kind, when it adds, 'A leetle black something foooll of what you need to buy things.'

Silence, as I search around for a helpful image to come to me.

'It sounds like money,' I think. 'But that is in my black *sac à main.*'

The truth suddenly dawns. It is the very bag he is talking about! It carries a vast amount of money (by my standard), all my credit cards, and a small electronic organiser, containing all my telephone and email contacts.

'*Oh, mon dieu!*' I exclaim, 'You're talking about my bag!'

'*Mais oui! Monsieur!*'

Within moments, he explains how he has found the bag in the middle of the road, and has activated my organiser to find the nearest telephone contact in his area, which, of course, happened to be my good friend Sylvia. And so he has traced me with his detective work.

When I have had time to calm down and stop kissing the phone, he suggests a meeting in a village halfway between his home and mine, and asks me to bring additional identification.

Thus it is that I pull up in a small parking area to see two men in suits waiting the other side of it. They are leaning on their vehicle, and straighten up as I get out. We approach each other, like drug dealers making a drop. They inspect my proof of identity as I inspect the contents of the bag. It is full of large denomination banknotes, which they ask me to count. Everything is there to the last franc.

Stammering my thanks, I immediately offer them a sizeable reward, which they wave aside with a delicate waft of their hands and a superior smile. I launch into a speech expressing relief, gratitude and appreciation of their honesty. They look at me, at each other and shrug to express their wonder that it could be otherwise. I eventually manage to thrust on them enough to buy wine, to celebrate my fortune at encountering such 'good eggs'. I almost bow, retreating backwards to my car. They wave me off and we separate in opposite directions, never to meet again.

I still reflect on the ingenuous nature of true honesty, which these men showed. The truth was, I had placed the bag on the roof of my car, while I packed tools and materials into the boot at a building centre, and then forgotten about it. It had obviously fallen off as I took the first bend on the road.

My friend Sylvia, never having known me by any name but Danby, had tremendous presence of mind to procure the telephone number. Had she not, I might never have retrieved my bag with its all too precious contents. Another blessing was to have been spared a nervous breakdown at the loss of the bag, for I was ignorant of it until the moment its return was assured.

As usual, the rough side of the coin, was having to explain to my wife how they came to find it. I concocted an excuse, saying my mind was distracted, I was under terrible stress from the problems caused by the renovation ... until it trailed away before her quizzical glance and sad shake of her head, which said quite clearly that I was the most undeservedly lucky person in the world.

And indeed I was. How can one not feel secure and safe among such people in the Charente?

So, would I advise others to take the same path and go out and rescue a French peasant's house? Would I do it again? Absolutely not! Not just because age makes it physically improbable and medically inadvisable, but even if I were in my prime, I would be certifiable if I took up the challenge, knowing what it really entails.

But that is it, isn't it? Would Michelangelo have painted the Sistine Chapel ceiling if he had considered the effect on his health? Would Scott have trotted off to the South Pole if he had known of his frozen end? Our ignorance is a great blessing.

If I can echo Noel Coward's advice to Mrs Worthington, when she informs him of her intention to put her daughter on the stage, 'Don't!'

If you follow this advice, you are clearly not passionate enough in your intention. But, if you are passionate enough, you will take no notice of it.

In that case, join with pride the honourable band of botchers.

Postscript

In the interests of privacy, I have withheld the name of the village, changed characters' names, and will deny all claims of recognition.

All fun is made with genuine respect and affection, and no more at others than at myself.

There is no intention to encourage people to rush off to chase their dreams. On the contrary, readers are advised to think twice, or indeed as many times as required, before doing so.